Free Cash Flow

Also by George C. Christy

Free Cash Flow: A Two-Hour Primer for Management and the Board

Founded in 1807, John Wiley & Sons is the oldest independent publishing company in the United States. With offices in North America, Europe, Australia and Asia, Wiley is globally committed to developing and marketing print and electronic products and services for our customers' professional and personal knowledge and understanding.

The Wiley Finance series contains books written specifically for finance and investment professionals as well as sophisticated individual investors and their financial advisors. Book topics range from portfolio management to e-commerce, risk management, financial engineering, valuation and financial instrument analysis, as well as much more.

For a list of available titles, visit our Web site at www.WileyFinance.com.

Free Cash Flow

*Seeing Through the Accounting Fog
Machine to Find Great Stocks*

GEORGE C. CHRISTY, CFA

WILEY

John Wiley & Sons, Inc.

Published by John Wiley & Sons, Inc., Hoboken, New Jersey.
Published simultaneously in Canada.

For general information on our other products and services or for technical support, please contact our Customer Care Department within the United States at (800) 762-2974, outside the United States at (317) 572-3993 or fax (317) 572-4002.

Wiley also publishes its books in a variety of electronic formats. Some content that appears in print may not be available in electronic books. For more information about Wiley products, visit our web site at www.wiley.com.

Library of Congress Cataloging-in-Publication Data:

Christy, George C.
  Free cash flow: seeing through the accounting fog machine to find great stocks/
George C. Christy.
    p. cm. – (Wiley finance series)
  Includes bibliographical references and index.
  ISBN 978-0-470-39175-4 (cloth/website)
  1. Cash flow.   2. Cash management.   3. Corporations–Cash position.   4. Investment analysis.   I. Title.
  HG4028.C45C539 2009
  332.63′22–dc22   2008033211

ISBN-13 978-0-470-39175-4

Printed in the United States of America

10   9   8   7   6   5   4   3   2   1

For my mother, Kathleen Stinchfield Christy
For my wife, Nobuko Miyachi Christy
For our son, Andrew
For our daughter, Anna and her husband, Evan

Contents

Foreword

In our recent book, *Free Cash Flow and Shareholder Yield: New Priorities for the Global Investor* (John Wiley & Sons, 2007), we offered a comprehensive introduction to the opportunities and challenges inherent in today's equity markets. By looking beyond the many obfuscations of traditional generally accepted accounting principles (GAAP) accounting, we endeavored to provide the informed investor with the tools necessary to navigate a changing investment landscape.

In George Christy's new book, *Free Cash Flow: Seeing Through the Accounting Fog Machine to Find Great Stocks*, the author brings these concepts to a new and eminently actionable level. In addition to providing practical definitions of difficult financial concepts, he teaches the investor/reader how to reengineer the accountant's obtuse financial statements into relevant snapshots of a company's capital productivity and free cash flow allocation.

The importance of understanding these concepts—free cash flow, in particular—cannot be overstated. For us, and for George Christy, free cash flow can be defined as the cash available for distribution to shareholders after all planned capital expenditures and all cash taxes. Within this definition, virtually all corporate strategies fall into one of five possible uses of free cash flow: cash dividends, share repurchases, debt paydowns, internal capital projects, and acquisitions. Knowing which strategy, or combination of strategies, to select is the key to increasing shareholder value. In this regard, Christy's insight is invaluable. He provides the reader with a clear, incisive, step-by-step methodology through which a company's historical stewardship of shareholder capital can be evaluated and its future commitment to responsible free cash flow deployment can be gauged.

The concept of free cash flow has always been important, but never more so than today. This is due to the changing orders of significance within the three sources of shareholder return. The following two exhibits show almost 80 years of decade-by-decade returns for the S&P 500.

The black line in these exhibits displays the rolling 10-year compound annual growth rate for the S&P 500 since 1936. If we disaggregate these returns into their three components—earnings per share (EPS) growth, dividend reinvestment, and changes to the price-earnings (P/E) ratio—we can see

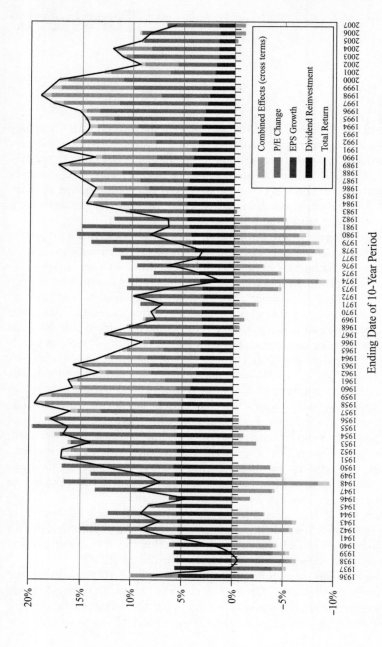

Components of Compound Annual Total Returns for Trailing 10-Year Periods (S&P 500 Index 1926–2007)
Sources: Epoch Investment Partners, Inc.; Standard & Poor's.

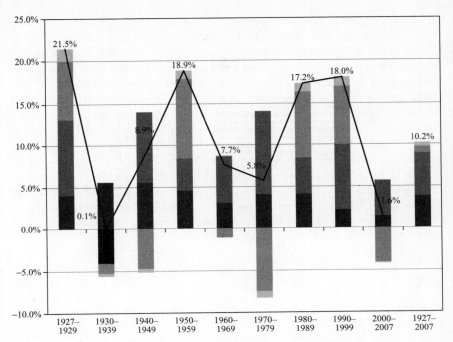

Components of Total Return by Decade *(S&P 500 Index 1927–2007)*
Sources: Epoch Investment Partners, Inc.; Standard & Poor's.

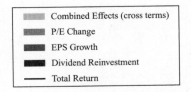

how the relative importance of each of these three drivers shifts throughout time. The 1980s and 1990s, for example, were characterized by the expansion of the P/E ratio or, conversely, by falling capitalization rates as applied to equities. Specifically, P/E ratios nearly quadrupled, providing almost half the equity return for the 20-year period between 1980 and 2000. This occurred because interest rates dropped from a high of more than 13 percent in the early 1980s to less than 4 percent by 2000, resulting in lower costs of capital.

Earnings and dividends mattered during this 20-year period, but they were of secondary importance. Today, the opposite is true. Going forward, P/E multiple expansion is unlikely to work in the investor's favor unless interest rates start trending downward. Therefore, it is safe to say that dividends and earnings are likely to account for nearly all of the returns in common stocks in the foreseeable future. And these two drivers come from one place: free cash flow. Never has free cash flow, and the investor's ability to recognize its efficient allocation, mattered more than it does right now.

It is under this crucial new investment rubric that George Christy has entered the scene. And, in our view, his timing—and his insights—could hardly be better. This book provides the reader with the concepts, the context, and the tools necessary to invest successfully in a global market that has become increasingly challenging for all investors, both institutional and individual. We applaud the author's efforts and recommend this book to all investors seeking shareholder value creation.

WILLIAM W. PRIEST
LINDSAY MCCLELLAND

For many decades GAAP earnings per share was the financial metric of choice of virtually all professional equity investors. Over the last decade, however, increasing problems with accrual accounting and a growing appreciation of investment economics have caused many professional investors to replace GAAP earnings with Free Cash Flow as their primary financial metric. Free Cash Flow is mentioned by buy-side investors and sell-side analysts in each issue of *Barron's* and on a daily basis on CNBC's market programs. Yet in spite of the rapidly growing popularity of Free Cash Flow, investors have not had recourse to a book that not only explains Free Cash Flow in detail but also shows how to use Free Cash Flow to increase investor return. This book does both. It also offers the reader a preformatted Excel worksheet that integrates the primary components of share value into an investor return model.

WHAT MAKES THIS BOOK UNIQUE

This book is not a long list of tips about investing. The book shows the investor how to use two new investment tools to find great stocks and increase investor return. The Free Cash Flow Statement© and the Free Cash Flow Worksheet© were created and developed by the author for this book. The Free Cash Flow Statement enables the investor to focus on the primary drivers of investor return: revenues, cash operating margin, and use of capital. The Free Cash Flow Worksheet is a preformatted Excel spreadsheet in which investors can do their own Free Cash Flow and investor return projections. In doing so, the Free Cash Flow Worksheet provides investors with an understandable, practical alternative to the discounted cash flow model used by many professional investors.

WHAT EACH CHAPTER DOES

Because this book is aimed at the widest possible audience, Chapter 1 begins with an explanation of some basic finance principles. It uses examples that anyone familiar with an income statement and a balance sheet can easily understand. Chapter 2 explains how GAAP accounting makes it difficult for investors to understand public companies' financial performance. Chapter 3 reconciles Free Cash Flow with GAAP earnings and describes the advantages of Free Cash Flow. Chapter 4 takes the reader step by step through the Free Cash Flow Statement. Chapter 5 explains how Free Cash Flow deployment can enhance or diminish investor return. Chapter 6 uses McDonald's 2004–2006 financials to lead the investor, row by row, through the Free Cash Flow Worksheet. After entering three years of selected data from McDonald's historical financial statements, we do a one-year projection of McDonald's Free Cash Flow and investor return. In Chapter 7, five other restaurant companies are compared to McDonald's and one another using both Free Cash Flow and GAAP metrics.

Chapter 8 shows the reader how to assess the CEO's commitment to investor return by analyzing three key information sources: the CEO annual letter to shareholders, the quarterly earnings conference call, and the CEO's incentive compensation package as described in the proxy. Chapter 9 provides guidance for the investor's initial foray into Free Cash Flow investing. Some of the topics addressed include finding stock candidates, screening, using the worksheet, and the CEO Exam.

WHO THE BOOK IS FOR

The book is for *experienced* investors. It is assumed the reader already follows an established due diligence process. The reader is expected to merge the book's Free Cash Flow and investor return analytics with the reader's existing due diligence discipline. Investors who read the book without using the Free Cash Flow Worksheet will no doubt enhance their understanding of Free Cash Flow and investor return. But by working with the Free Cash Flow Worksheet with, say, just 5 or 10 companies, the reader will develop a much deeper understanding of the benefits and limitations of Free Cash Flow investing. There is no guidance in the book on using Excel. Readers without Excel experience are on their own.

In addition to investors, the book's intended readers include:

- Clients of investment management firms
- Training programs of investment management firms
- CEOs, CFOs, and board members of public companies
- CEO and CFO candidates
- Corporate managers, division heads, vice presidents
- Management training programs
- Business schools

WHAT THE BOOK IS NOT

The book is definitely not appropriate as an introduction to equity investing. It does not cover all aspects of equity investing. Its focus is narrow but intense: analyzing a company's financial performance from the equity investor's vantage point. The Free Cash Flow Worksheet is not appropriate for use on financial companies such as banks, brokerage firms, insurance companies, or REITs. Financial companies' capital structures and specialized accounting require a specialized approach, just as a specialized approach is required for a GAAP analysis of financial companies.

A DIFFERENT PERSPECTIVE

The vast majority of "how-to-invest" books are written by professional investors. These authors have spent their careers looking at public companies from the outside. Their access to public companies is limited to the companies' public disclosures and other publicly available information. Their books consist primarily of investing tips often in the form of do's and don'ts. Those authors also talk at length about their biggest stock winners (and sometimes losers). By carefully picking and choosing from these menus of tips and tales, investors hope to enhance their stock-picking skills and improve their equity returns.

This book is not written by a professional investor. The author was most recently the treasurer of a public company. For over 30 years before that, he was a corporate banker in Chicago, Tokyo, and Los Angeles. In the course of his banking career, he worked with hundreds of CEOs, CFOs, and board members. To a certain extent, the author's perspective is skewed by his banking experience, which included numerous contests with CEOs and CFOs over the division of limited cash flows between lender and borrower. Because bank loans are repaid by cash flow, not by GAAP earnings, the author learned early in his career how to analyze cash flow. After his banking years, the author was a consultant at one of the country's largest investor relations firms. He wrote clients' quarterly earnings press releases, annual reports and corporate profiles. He also helped client CEOs and CFOs prepare for quarterly earnings conference calls and presentations to investor conferences and meetings.

Throughout his career, the author has been an insider, privy to financial and other confidential information about the companies he has worked with as a banker, consultant, or Treasurer. Furthermore, the author's career gave him an insider's appreciation of how CEOs and CFOs manage their companies, their public disclosures, and their relationships with the Street.

The author does not claim to offer an approach to equity investing that is either superior to those articulated elsewhere or will, if replicated by the reader, result in unlimited wealth and fortune. The author does offer an insider's perspective on cash flow investing that is different from that of the typical equity money manager. Different is not always better, but those investors looking for great stocks should gain new insights and understanding of how to see through the accounting fog machine with Free Cash Flow.

All calculations and statements in this book exclude the return impact of commissions, taxes, and other direct and indirect transaction costs.

The abstract paintings of Jackson Pollock created a lot of controversy in the art world of the 1950s. Pollock's paintings appeared to some observers to be the result of someone hurling paint cans of randomly chosen colors at a large canvas. One afternoon at a Manhattan gallery's exhibition of his paintings, Pollock wandered alone through the gallery's rooms. He encountered a slightly inebriated street person, seeking refuge from a thunderstorm, standing in front of one of Pollock's colorful works.

The street person looked at Pollock and exclaimed, "This is ridiculous! Any idiot could have done this!"

Pollock glanced at his painting and then turned to the street person and said, "You're absolutely right. Anyone could have done this, but no one ever did."

CHAPTER 1

Investing 101

You and I are 50/50 partners in a private equity firm. A friend of ours owns a small manufacturing company that makes outdoor furniture. He wants to retire and has asked us if we would be interested in buying his company. Annual sales are $75 million and he has about 150 employees. He has developed a good management team that will remain after the company is sold. While the U.S. furniture manufacturing industry has been hard hit by low-cost imports, our friend's business appears to be doing very well. After a tour of the plant and product showroom, we decide it is a good idea to spend some time on an analysis of the company's business and its financial statements. Our due diligence analysis is focused on one question: What is the likely return we'll receive on our investment if we buy the outdoor furniture company?

Our investment return from the outdoor furniture company equals the sum of:

1. The difference between the price we pay for the company and the price we receive when we sell it, divided by the price we paid; plus
2. Whatever cash we remove from the company

The cash we take out of the company would be dividends we decide to pay to our firm.

PRICE

The price, both when we buy the company and when we sell it, is primarily determined by two things:

1. The amount of future cash flow the buyer expects the company to generate after the sale closes and
2. The general level of interest rates at the time of the transaction

While we must analyze the company's historical cash flows to understand the company's business, when we buy a company we are not buying its *historical* cash flows. We are buying our right to the company's *future* cash flows. The outdoor furniture company's future cash flows can be divided into two time periods. The first time period is while we own the company. The company's cash flows while we own it will determine how much cash, if any, we can remove from the company to reinvest or spend as we see fit. The second time period is after we sell the company. Our buyer will estimate the company's future cash flows and will agree to pay us a price that enables the buyer to obtain the total return the buyer needs in the years after buying the company. *Cash flow*, unfortunately, is a term that means different things to different people. We will define Free Cash Flow in the next section. The general level of interest rates affects prices of investments. The higher the expected inflation rate during our investment term, the lower the price we should pay for an investment's future cash flows because there will be fewer goods and services we will be able to purchase with the proceeds (dividends plus the net sale proceeds) of our investment. The lower the anticipated inflation rate, the higher the price we can afford to pay without a decline in the future purchasing power of our investment proceeds.

FREE CASH FLOW

When we purchase 100 percent of a company, we are acquiring the right to all of the company's future surplus or Free Cash Flow. By *surplus* and *free* we mean whatever cash remains after the company:

1. Uses cash to pay its operating costs such as employee salaries, wages and benefits, suppliers, utility bills, legal and accounting fees, taxes, interest on debt if any, and so forth
2. Uses cash to extend credit terms to customers and to build inventory, and
3. Uses cash to buy equipment, computers, vehicles, land, and buildings

Once the company has taken care of its obligations in items 1, 2, and 3, the owners—that would be us if we buy the company—can pretty much do what we want with the Free Cash Flow because it is our company. It is not management's company. Management has little or no equity at risk. Management is compensated by salary and bonuses while we depend entirely on our investment return for our compensation. We can tell management to use the company's Free Cash Flow to pay dividends to our firm, to buy other companies if we decide that is a smart thing to do, to repay debt if there is any or to buy back the company's stock.

Now that we have introduced Free Cash Flow, we can refine our definition of investment return by replacing *cash flow* with *Free Cash Flow.* Our investment return, then, is (1) the difference between the purchase price and the sale price (both of which are determined by expected Free Cash Flow), divided by the purchase price and (2) the amount of the company's Free Cash Flow we decide to pay as dividends to ourselves. Each cash dollar the company spends on its operating costs, customer receivables, inventory, new equipment, new buildings, and other purchases is one less dollar of Free Cash Flow. And one dollar less of Free Cash Flow means less return for us, the owners, because investing is a cash business. We invest cash to buy the furniture company. We expect to receive a cash return on our investment. A Net Income return does not help us because our bank does not accept Net Income deposits. Now that we have defined Free Cash Flow, we can get started on determining the price we are willing to pay for the company.

RISK AND RETURN

We use the yields on U.S. Treasury securities to help us set a ballpark purchase price for the outdoor furniture company. A risk assessment of Treasuries is elementary. If the U.S. Treasury cannot return our principal and interest in full and on time, then our money probably is not worth anything anyway. Say we are thinking of owning and running the furniture company for about 10 years. The company generates $10 million of annual Free Cash Flow and is expected to do as well or better over the next few years. We are confident we can cut some costs and reduce capital utilization. To be conservative, we will ignore any such improvements as well as any sales growth potential in our analysis. Assume the 10-year Treasuries are currently yielding 5 percent. Ignoring the effect of interest reinvestment, that is 5 percent of virtually risk-free Free Cash Flow each year for 10 years followed by the return at maturity of 100 percent of our investment. Given all of the risks involved in owning our new company, it is obvious that our anticipated return on our investment in the outdoor furniture company must be substantially higher than the 10-year Treasuries' 5 percent yield. What if the company were overwhelmed by new competitors and vaporized in three years? We would be left with nothing but the furniture on our patio.

THE RETURN MULTIPLE

We need to decide *how much* riskier we think our investment in the furniture company is likely to be compared to an investment of the same amount and maturity in U.S. Treasuries. Do we think the purchase of the company is two times, four times, or 10 times riskier than buying Treasuries? Let's say we think ownership of the outdoor furniture company would be at least four times riskier than owning Treasuries. A 4× Return Multiple means we should be getting four times the Treasuries' annual 5 percent return, or an annual return of about 20 percent from owning the outdoor furniture company. Many investors expect around a 15 percent return on public company stocks. Our friend's company is a small private company, so its shares are much less liquid than the shares of a public company. That additional risk suggests a 20 percent return target is not way out of line. As we learn more about the company in our due diligence, we can adjust our Return Multiple up or down if we learn the company's business offers more or less risk than our original estimate.

RETURN AND PRICE

We now know our required return on investment is roughly 20 percent. What price should we pay to generate a 20 percent annual return on our investment in the furniture company? Let's start with the formula for the simple annual yield, or return, of any investment:

$$\text{Return on Investment} = \frac{\text{Annual Free Cash Flow}}{\text{Investment}} \qquad (1.1)$$

The price we pay for the company is the investment in the formula above. To calculate the investment, we divide $10 million of Free Cash Flow by our required 20 percent return and get an investment, or price, of $50 million:

$$\text{Investment} = \frac{\text{Annual Free Cash Flow}}{\text{Required Return}} = \frac{\$10\text{ million}}{20\%} = \$50\text{ million} \qquad (1.2)$$

To keep things as simple as possible, we are not incorporating the time value of money in our calculations. Our investment return formula incorporates:

1. The expected Free Cash Flows generated by the investment
2. The price we are paying for the investment

3. The market's perception of future risk-free interest rate levels for 10 years
4. The relative risk of the investment (the risk relative to 10-year Treasuries)

Our 4× Return Multiple incorporates items (3) and (4). Our assessment of an investment's ability to generate Free Cash Flow is our critical starting point because we are investing cash and we want to receive our return in cash. Equally critical is the price we pay for the investment. If we overpay for a company, even for a company with outstanding Free Cash Flow prospects, we may not get our expected return. If we pay $60 million for the company, our return will be 18.75 percent, not 20 percent. Or, in other words, a $60 million price would give us a 20 percent return on the first $50 million. What would our return be on the last $10 million? It would be a zero percent return.

By applying our required 4× Return Multiple to the current Treasuries' yield for the appropriate term, we are reflecting the market's expectation of the inflation rate during the term of our investment. Again, the higher the expected inflation rate during our investment term, the lower the price we should pay for the Free Cash Flow we are buying because there will be fewer goods and services we will be able to purchase with the proceeds (dividends plus net sale proceeds) of our investment. The lower the anticipated inflation rate, the higher the price we can afford to pay without a decline in the future purchasing power of our investment proceeds. By comparing our investment's risk to Treasuries in the Return Multiple, we are attempting to ensure we are sufficiently rewarded for the incremental risk we are taking in our equity investment as compared to our investment in Treasuries. We are taking a lot more risk when we buy stocks and we must receive a lot more return. Comparing our expected return on our acquisition opportunity to a Treasuries' yield may at first seem strange. Our entire analysis is cash-based. We are investing cash and we expect to receive a cash return. We measure our investment's value by its Free Cash Flow generation and so we must use a cash benchmark return.

The Return Multiple provides yet another benefit. It helps us manage the chances of paying too much for stocks. This is especially important at the peak of strong equity markets when many investors are overpaying for stocks. In that type of market climate, dependence on comparative Price-to-Earnings ratios (PEs)—almost all of which are too high—leads to rude disappointments. Like all financial metrics, the Return Multiple is by no means foolproof. In periods of financial market turbulence, the utility of interest rates as a proxy for future inflation is sometimes diminished. But the Return Multiple does help us take a step back, assess a company's expected Free Cash Flows in the context of the relative risk and return of alternative investments, and ask: Does this investment really make sense? Well, we offered our friend $50 million for the furniture company and he accepted. Now that we are the owners, we have some decisions to make, but first we need to understand what other financial variables affect our return on investment.

DEBT

Most companies at some time need more cash than they are generating in Free Cash Flow. Our furniture company may need to make significant increases in customer credit and inventory because of seasonal fluctuations in the business. Or it may need additional cash for receivables and inventory if it is rapidly expanding the scale of its operations. We may decide to expand manufacturing or service capacity by building a new plant or by opening new stores. If we, the owners, are not able or willing to invest additional cash in the company to meet its needs, then the company must try to obtain the required cash by borrowing from a bank. There are two ways the company's use of debt can increase or reduce our investment return.

The first way is the loan interest cost. Let's say we want to build a new plant that will cost $5 million and it will take one year to build. The new plant is expected to generate $1 million of annual Free Cash Flow in addition to the company's current Free Cash Flow of $10 million. Also assume that none of the $10 million in Free Cash Flow is available to fund the new plant (you and I are both building new houses and we need all the cash we can get our hands on). Adding the $1 million increase to the existing $10 million makes $11 million in total Free Cash Flow in the year after the plant is finished. That represents a 10 percent increase in Free Cash Flow. If the company's use of the loan proceeds results in increased Free Cash Flow after the loan interest has been paid to the bank, our investment return will benefit from the use of debt. Our return will benefit from higher future Free Cash Flows because: (1) we will be able to take more cash out of the company if we want to, (2) we will have more options to grow the company by using its Free Cash Flow for new capacity or acquisitions, and (3) the higher Free Cash Flow will hopefully persuade our eventual buyer that the company's future Free Cash Flows are likely to be higher. Recall that interest on debt is included in the operating costs enumerated in the definition of Free Cash Flow provided earlier. Case 1 on the next page assumes no plant is built. Case 2 and 3 assume the plant is built and has been in operation for one year.

Case 1

- Company has no debt. No plant is built.
- Free Cash Flow is $10 million.

Case 2

- Company has borrowed $5 million at 10 percent interest (after tax benefit) to build a new plant.
- Loan interest is $500,000 ($5 million × 10 percent).
- New plant has increased Free Cash Flow by $1 million (excluding $500,000 interest on bank loan).

Free Cash Flow	$11.0 million (excluding interest)
Less	0.5 million interest
Net Free Cash Flow	$10.5 million (including interest)

Case 3

- Company has borrowed $5 million at 10 percent interest (after tax benefit) to build new plant.
- Loan interest is $500,000 ($5 million × 10 percent).
- New plant has increased Free Cash Flow by $0.2 million (excluding $500,000 interest on bank loan).

Free Cash Flow	$10.2 million (excluding interest)
Less	0.5 million interest
Net Free Cash Flow	$9.7 million (including interest)

Everything else being equal, Case 2 appears to be better than Case 1 and Case 3. In Case 2, the Net Free Cash Flow generated by the new plant covers the interest cost on the new debt. If our investment in our plant cannot cover its interest cost, why would we want to build the plant? In Case 3, the new plant, for whatever reason(s), increases Free Cash Flow by only $200,000. That increase does not cover the $500,000 interest cost. If that is our best judgment, we should probably rethink a new plant.

The interest our company must pay on the bank loan is one of the two ways debt can affect our return on investment. Here's the second way. Let's say we decide we must sell the company three years after the plant opens but *before* the bank loan has been repaid in full. If the debt has not been

repaid in full by the time we sell the company, the cash purchase payment
we receive from the buyer of our company will be reduced by the balance of
the company's debt. That is because our bank must be repaid in full at the
sale's closing. Our bank's decision to make a loan to our company assumed
we would continue to be the company's owners and our management team
would stay on. If the company is going to have new owners, the bank wants
its loan repaid. The same thing happens when we sell a house. In the escrow
closing, we receive whatever is left of the sale price after our mortgage lender
has been paid in full and all transaction costs have been paid by the escrow
company. If our company's use of the loan proceeds resulted in a higher
assessment by the buyer of our company's future Free Cash Flows (and
therefore resulted in a higher price), *and* the amount of that higher price
exceeded the loan balance at closing, our return on investment would likely
benefit from borrowing the funds. If, on the other hand, the loan balance
exceeded the amount of the price increase, our cash proceeds from the sale
escrow would be less than it would have been had we not built the plant.
We will use the Case 1 and Case 2 numbers again and relabel them Case 4
and Case 5, respectively.

Case 4

- Company has no debt. No plant is built.
- Free Cash Flow is $10 million.
- Our buyer's required annual Return on Investment is 18 percent.
- We sell the company for $55.6 million.

$$\text{Price} = \frac{\text{Annual Free Cash Flow}}{\text{Buyer's Required Return}} = \frac{\$10 \text{ million}}{18\%} = \$55.6 \text{ million}$$

$$(1.3)$$

- We receive cash proceeds (net of $1.6 million transaction costs) of $54 million.

Sale Price	$55.6 million
Less	1.6 million transaction costs
Cash Proceeds	$54.0 million

Case 5

- Company has borrowed $5 million at 10 percent interest (after tax benefit) to build new plant.

- New plant has increased Free Cash Flow by $1 million (excluding $500,000 interest on bank loan).

Free Cash Flow	$11.0 million (excluding interest)
Less	0.5 million interest
Net Free Cash Flow	$10.5 million (including interest)

- Three years later, we sell the company to a buyer whose required annual Return on Investment is 18 percent.
- We sell the company for $61.1 million.
- The loan balance is $4 million. Because the loan is repaid in full at the sale escrow, the buyer excludes the $400,000 interest cost and uses a Free Cash Flow number of $11 million.

$$\text{Price} = \frac{\text{Annual Free Cash Flow}}{\text{Buyer's Required Return}} = \frac{\$11 \text{ million}}{18\%} = \$61.1 \text{ million}$$

$$(1.4)$$

- We receive cash proceeds (net of loan payoff and transaction costs) of $55.5 million.

Sale Price	$61.1 million
Less	1.6 million transaction costs
Less	4.0 million loan balance
Cash Proceeds	$55.5 million

Investors must understand how *all* of the key financial variables influence investor return. The cash proceeds in Case 5 turn out to be higher than the cash proceeds in Case 1, the no-plant scenario. But what if the loan balance at closing is higher? What if the new plant performs poorly and generates no incremental Free Cash Flow? Debt can enable a company to accomplish good things but it does carry risks for the owners and investors.

EQUITY

What if our company is unable to borrow the needed funds from a bank? Perhaps the local banks are not interested in adding to their exposure to manufacturing companies. Or maybe the banks have so many problem loans they do not want to add new borrowers. If new debt is not an option, the company may be able to sell new shares of common stock to new shareholders. If we think our company can use the new cash received from the sale of stock to increase the company's future Free Cash Flow by a greater percentage than the percentage increase in the number of shares outstanding resulting from the stock sale, then issuing new shares may well be a good idea.

We again use our example of the $5 million new plant. The new plant is expected to generate an incremental $10 million in Free Cash Flow. If we think we can raise $5 million in new equity while increasing the total number of shares by less than 10 percent, our investment return should benefit. But if we have to give up more than 10 percent of the company to attract $5 million of new equity, we are going to lose some return because our Free Cash Flow per share will decline. Assuming the company currently has 10 million shares of common stock, here is the math:

Case 6

We have 100 percent ownership of 10 million shares:

$$\text{Free Cash Flow per share} = \frac{\text{Annual Free Cash Flow}}{\text{Number of Shares}} = \frac{\$10 \text{ million}}{10 \text{ million}} = \$1 \tag{1.5}$$

Case 7

After selling 500,000 new shares to investors for $5 million and the new plant is up and running for one year:

$$\text{Free Cash Flow per share} = \frac{\text{Annual Free Cash Flow}}{\text{Number of Shares}}$$
$$= \frac{\$11 \text{ million}}{10.5 \text{ million}} = \$1.05 \tag{1.6}$$

Case 8

After selling 1.5 million shares to investors for $5 million and the new plant is up and running for one year:

$$\text{Free Cash Flow per share} = \frac{\text{Annual Free Cash Flow}}{\text{Number of Shares}}$$
$$= \frac{\$11 \text{ million}}{11.5 \text{ million}} = \$0.96 \tag{1.7}$$

If the plant is less successful than anticipated, then we will see a lower-than-anticipated Free Cash Flow per share. Sales and net income may be higher after the new plant is running but if the end result is lower Free Cash Flow per share, then the value of our equity investment has declined.

In any event, because we would be bringing in additional investors to the company's equity ownership, we must now shift our focus from the company's *total* Free Cash Flow to its Free Cash Flow *per share*. Before, our private equity firm was the 100 percent owner and our focus was therefore on the company's total Free Cash Flow. But if the company is going to have multiple owners, whether it is a private or public company, we must shift our primary focus to Free Cash Flow per share because changes in the amount of Free Cash Flow and in the total number of shares that divide up the company's Free Cash Flow affect the value of our shares in the company.

DEBT VERSUS EQUITY

If we know we can fund the new plant with either debt or with new stock, how do we determine whether debt or new equity would have the more favorable impact on our investment return? We would do the same type of new debt analysis and new equity analysis we have just done to see how each affects incremental Free Cash Flow per share. The debt route will often increase Free Cash Flow per share more than the equity route because with new debt we would not be issuing new common stock shares. If we went with debt, our existing 10 million shares would enjoy all of the incremental benefits (and costs) of the new plants. Debt interest is an incremental cost not incurred with new equity, but such interest is at least tax deductible. Yet debt involves certain risks the company would not face were it to choose new equity. We want to be sure our company will be able to pay the interest and principal to the lenders as required by the repayment schedule. We would need to build a cushion in the loan repayment schedule so that when unexpected setbacks occur in the business, our company will have enough cash to meet the repayment schedule. And do not forget what happens if we must sell the company before the debt is repaid. The loan balance is deducted from our sale proceeds. If that occurs before the expected incremental Free Cash Flows have materialized (or at least are judged by the buyer to be a given), our investment return may well suffer. We have already hit on three financial variables that affect our investment return: expected Free Cash Flow, the number of shares, and the amount of debt. As investors, we are very concerned about these three numbers. We are even more concerned about the expected changes in these numbers because it is really *the future changes* in these three numbers and several other variables that determine our returns.

PRIVATE COMPANY VERSUS PUBLIC COMPANY

The outdoor furniture company is a private company. As the only owners of a private company, we have full control over all the major business decisions, including the disposition of the company's Free Cash Flow. Therefore, our analysis of our expected return on investment focuses on the furniture company as a whole: its total Free Cash Flow, its total dividend payments, its total debt, and so forth.

As owners of public company shares, however, we have no control over anything other than the price at which we buy and sell our shares (setting aside shareholder voting rights and proxy fights, and so on). Our only decision is to accept or not accept the market price. Because we are buying and selling shares, we must focus our analysis on changes in the value of each share, not just the changes in the company's overall financial results and parameters. But other than our *per share* focus, our analysis of our public company shares will be essentially the same analysis we used in analyzing our furniture company investment.

We are investing cash in public company shares to obtain a cash return. If we are a buyer, we will buy the public company's shares at the market price if our analysis suggests the company's expected Free Cash Flow per share when combined with the impact of other expected changes in the company's finances (such as debt levels and dividends) will give us our *required return* on investment. The Return Multiple can help us define *required*. If we own the stock, we will sell the stock if our analysis suggests the company's future performance will not enable us to meet our required return on investment.

This book's objective is to provide the investor with the tools needed to determine if a public company's common stock is likely to meet the required return on investment. To estimate a company's future Free Cash Flow, we first need to understand its historical and current Free Cash Flows. Fortunately for investors, the SEC requires public companies to provide financial statements each quarter. Unfortunately for investors, the SEC mandates financial statements be prepared in accordance with generally accepted accounting principles (GAAP). If we think of GAAP as a pyramid of rules, the bottom of the pyramid is occupied by the rules of accrual accounting. The rest of the pyramid consists of rules that dictate how public companies apply accrual accounting in preparing financial statements. Now, that is all well and good except for one problem. The primary purpose of accrual accounting makes our focus on Free Cash Flow somewhat more challenging than necessary. But challenges are fun. And more important, investors who surmount challenges often hold an advantage over those investors who do not even know the challenges exist. What, then, is the primary purpose of accrual accounting?

CHAPTER 2

The Accounting Fog Machine

The primary purpose of accrual accounting is to hide the cash flow. Before accrual accounting came along, companies kept their books on a cash basis only. The company's bookkeepers kept track of the cash coming into the company from customers and the cash going out to employees, suppliers and others. A company's financial results equaled the difference between the cash in and the cash out. For example, when a piece of equipment was purchased for $50,000 in cash, the transaction was booked as a decrease in cash of $50,000 and a reduction of $50,000 in operating results for the period in which the equipment was purchased. Most people were generally satisfied with cash books. They were easy for companies to maintain and easy for outside users, such as creditors and lenders, to understand.

Over time some bookkeepers and some creditors came to believe cash books were inherently misleading. They thought unless a company's costs (such as the $50,000 piece of equipment) were *matched* with the company's Revenues made possible by those costs, the outsider looking at the company's financials would be misled as to the company's "real" financial condition. This matching concept is the basis for today's accrual accounting.

Generally Accepted Accounting Principles (GAAP) require a company to distribute the cost of the $50,000 piece of equipment over the years in which the equipment contributes to Revenues. So instead of the entire $50,000 being deducted from operating results in the year in which the equipment is acquired, the company deducts, say, $5,000 each year in a Depreciation charge against earnings because the company believes the equipment will have a productive life of 10 years. How do they know the useful life is 10 years? They may or may not know. If it is a new type of machine, they may not know if the useful life is 5, 10, or 15 years. In any event, the accountants assert a company's supplier would have a distorted perception of a company's financial condition if the supplier were to look at the company's cash book financials for the year in which the entire $50,000 equipment purchase were deducted. The accountants say an outsider would probably conclude the $50,000 hit against operating results meant the company's condition was much worse than it actually was. Similarly, when the supplier looks at the company's operating results in the years *after* the year in which the $50,000 equipment was acquired, the accountants argue the supplier would probably conclude the company was in better condition than it actually was because the cost associated with the equipment was not reflected in the operating results of the years following the equipment purchase.

The accountants believe the reduced transparency and extensive use of estimates that are inherent in accrual accounting are more than compensated for by the apparent stability and continuity of a company's operating results. But hiding the cash flow under a fog of useful life assumptions and other estimates trades the reality of cash flows for a smoothed and averaged hypothetical aggregate: GAAP Earnings Per Share (EPS). Remember, we are investing cash to get a cash return. *Accurate* accounting estimates make it difficult enough for cash flow investors to understand a company's cash flows. Inaccurate estimates compound the challenge.

If Depreciation were the only cost allocation, cash flow investors would have it relatively easy. But there are countless accruals and allocations besides Depreciation in the thousands and thousands of the FASB's rule pages: bad debts, warranty costs, restructuring, inventory obsolescence, pension fund, customer discount estimates, and countless more. While many individual accruals and allocations may be too small to matter, accruals in the aggregate are often material in their impact on a company's Earnings Per Share. We will show you a graph to this point in a later chapter.

GAAP: COMPETING THEORIES, MATTERS OF OPINION, POLITICAL COMPROMISES

GAAP's problems are not limited to accruals. As Alex J. Pollock of the American Enterprise Institute points out, ". . . every calculation of net profit reflects choices from among competing theories of accounting. None of these theories is simply the truth. Like theories of politics, they depend on inherently imprecise ideas such as fairness, reasonableness, value, being appropriate under the circumstances, and future usefulness. They are in important respects matters of opinion and philosophy, not matters of fact or mathematical truth."[1] Mr. Pollock also says: ". . . [A]ccounting standards are often hotly contentious among the interested parties and the final form of accounting standards is the result of complicated political compromises."[2] He continues: "Disputes over accounting standards often involve corporations, trade associations, accounting firms, and academics split among opposing sides, splits within the FASB itself, pressure from the SEC, interventions from Congress and, occasionally, legislation."[3] And

Mr. Pollock cautions: "Hence the eternal verity of the investment proverb, 'Profit is an opinion; cash is a fact.'"[4]

GAAP: ACCRUAL ABUSE

David Henry's outstanding *Business Week* article, "Fuzzy Numbers," is one of the best reviews in recent years of accrual abuses *permitted* by GAAP.[5]

> *According to . . . Richard G. Sloan of the University of Michigan Business School and Scott Richardson of the University of Pennsylvania's Wharton School, . . . companies making the largest (accrual) estimates—and thus reporting the most overstated earnings—initially attract investors like moths to a flame. Later, when the estimates prove overblown, their stocks founder. They lag, on average, stocks of similar companies by 10 percentage points a year, costing investors more than $100 billion in market returns. These companies . . . have higher incidences of earnings restatements, SEC enforcement actions, and accounting related lawsuits, notes Neil Baron, chairman of Criterion Research Group. . . .*

GAAP: ERRORS BRED BY COMPLEXITY

GAAP's complexity makes financial statements unreliable. GAAP's maze of rules results in unintentional errors by companies. A recent op-ed piece in the *Wall Street Journal* written by Kenneth Wilcox, a public company CEO, says that: ". . . [N]either companies nor auditors can really understand all of the primary accounting pronouncements coming out of the FASB, the number of which has gone from 104 in 1989 to 159 today. Many of them are 50 pages or more in length with accompanying interpretations that may be 10 times as long as the pronouncement itself."[6] In 2005, almost 1,200 public companies had to issue restatements of their GAAP financials. These restatements were issued after the CEO and CFO signed off on the original financials, after the outside auditors signed off, after the Board of Directors signed off, after the quarterly earnings press release was issued, after the 10-Q was filed and after shares were bought and sold on the basis of the reported yet flawed financial statements. These 1,200 public companies had to issue 1,796 separate corrections to their financial statements. Setting aside the tax effects of the 1,796 corrections, how many of the corrections affected actual cash flow? Probably none, or close to none. And these were presumably unintentional errors.

GAAP'S GAP

What about intentional distortions? Most companies try hard to be sensible and faithful to investors' needs in the preparation of their financial statements. But there are some management teams that exploit GAAP's flexibility for self-serving reasons and do massive damage to investor returns. Recall accounting scandals such as Enron, WorldCom, Tyco, Adelphia, Xerox, Sunbeam, Krispy Kreme, and Rite Aid. These and other examples of nefarious accounting schemes are clearly described in Cecil W. Jackson's *Business Fairy Tales* (in Recommended Reading). There will always be CEOs and CFOs who break the rules, whatever the rules are. If the SEC were to require public companies to issue Cash Receipts and Disbursement Reports each quarter, investors would more quickly catch some rule breakers.

GAAP EPS: AN INCOMPLETE DEFINITION OF FINANCIAL PERFORMANCE

This important deficiency in GAAP is usually ignored by "how-to-invest" authors. For a company to produce a return for investors, the company must generate sustainable Free Cash Flow. Recall that Free Cash Flow is cash available for investors after the company has funded its cash costs, its receivables and inventory, and its capital expenditures. A company's GAAP net income, also called *profit* or *earnings,* not only includes many noncash costs but also ignores the use of cash for receivables, inventory, and capital expenditures. Yes, net income includes the Depreciation expense for capital expenditures, but there can be significant differences between a company's Depreciation expense and the amount of cash used for capital expenditures. Therefore, GAAP Earnings Per Share is an incomplete statement of financial performance.

GAAP EPS: INVESTING IN AN ECONOMIC VACUUM

Chapter 1 noted the critical importance of interest rates to investor return. In general, the more interest rates increase, the more likely price inflation will increase, the less will be the purchasing power of an investment's future cash flow, and therefore the lower the price we should offer to pay for an investment. Without question, accountants are smart, hard-working professionals. But by moving away from cash flow, accountants have made it more difficult for investors to assess returns and compare the returns of alternative investments. Because GAAP earnings is a noncash number, calculating investment yields using GAAP earnings per share is economic nonsense. Why do we invest? We invest to gain a cash return to have more cash to spend on things or to give to charity or to our family or friends. GAAP earnings cannot be invested. GAAP earnings cannot be spent. We cannot use GAAP earnings per share in an investment yield calculation because it makes no sense to apply interest rates to a noncash number. If we cannot incorporate interest rates in our investment analysis of a company's stock, how can we legitimately anchor our return analysis to the relative return and relative risk of alternative investments such as corporate bonds or Treasuries? If we cannot do that, we are investing in an economic vacuum.

EBITDA IS NOT A CASH FLOW METRIC

A newspaper columnist recently referred to a cable TV industry valuation analysis by a prominent buy-side analyst. The analyst argued that cable industry valuations were very low based on the companies' EBITDA multiples. EBITDA (Earnings Before Interest, Taxes, Depreciation, and Amortization) is frequently used as a cash flow proxy in structuring acquisitions and other corporate finance transactions. EBITDA is a dangerous proxy for cash flow because (1) EBITDA includes noncash items in the "Earnings" component; (2) EBITDA excludes cash required for Working Capital and (3) EBITDA excludes cash required for capital expenditures. Presumably both the excluded Working Capital and the excluded capital expenditures are assumed to be needed to reach the projected Revenues that generate the projected Earnings. Those who rely on EBITDA are essentially saying it does not make any difference whether a company generating $100 million in operating income requires $20 million or $40 million in additional Working Capital and capital expenditures to increase sales by 20 percent. How can an industry valuation analysis ignore the capital required for Working Capital and fixed assets? And to top it all off, we are talking about cable TV—a capital-intensive industry. It is hard to imagine a good reason to use EBITDA. True, investment bankers like to use EBITDA when pitching an acquisition deal to a CEO because EBITDA makes complicated things sound simple.

THE GAAP CASH FLOW STATEMENT

GAAP's Cash Flow Statement is a cash flow *in name only*. Yes, the Consolidated Statement of Cash Flows provides critical information not provided by the income statement such as the period's Depreciation expense and investment in new plant, equipment, and other long-term assets (Capital Expenditures, or *Capex*). But the GAAP Statement of Cash Flows has several serious problems. GAAP allows companies substantial latitude in choosing into which of the Cash Flow Statement's three sections—Operating, Investing, or Financing—they put an item. An example: Some companies classify insurance reimbursements for fixed asset losses (resulting from a fire or flood, and so forth) in the Operating section rather than in the Investing section and some companies do the reverse. Another example: In 2005, some Fortune 500 companies were ordered by the SEC to reclassify the sale of their captive finance units' receivables from the Investing section to the Operating section, thereby reducing "Cash provided from operating activities." Another example: If a company sells a division and receives a tax benefit from the sale, that tax benefit appears in the Operating section rather than in the Investing section. Another example: A company that finances new equipment with a capital lease is not required to include the cost of the new equipment in either the capital expenditures line in the Investing section or in the Financing section. The amount must be disclosed in a footnote. The last example: So many public companies had been incorrectly classifying cash flow from discontinued operations that the SEC in early 2006 was forced to allow companies to issue corrections that required no earnings' restatements. There are many, many more examples. The flexibility companies enjoy in deciding into which of the three Cash Flow sections they put an item is one of GAAP's biggest failings. This subject is covered in depth in *Creative Cash Flow Reporting: Uncovering Sustainable Financial Performance* by Charles W. Mulford and Eugene E. Comiskey. This excellent book is listed in the Recommended Readings appendix.

BEWARE THE BALANCE SHEET

Please consider some advice from a banker who has not only looked at countless balance sheets but has also toured the companies' operations; interrogated management about their business, industry, competition, products and services, strengths, and weaknesses; and analyzed both the financial statements *and* confidential company reports. Some examples of confidential reports are an accounts receivable aging (how many dollars of receivables are current, past due 30 days, past due 60 days, and so on), an inventory aging, a detailed Capex schedule (how Capex is allocated to various projects and to maintenance) and an accounts payable aging. Of course, the key report for bankers is the company's confidential cash flow projection because cash, not Net Income, pays interest and repays loans. Having seen the significant differences between (a) the balance sheets' portrayal of companies' financial condition and (b) the reality of the companies' financial condition, here is some humble advice: Do not make investment decisions based on a company's balance sheet or any item(s) therein other than the Cash and Marketable Securities accounts. Hopefully the following quick tour of the balance sheet illuminates some of the many problems lurking underneath the balance sheet.

LIQUIDITY

Too many investors draw too many flawed conclusions from balance sheet accounts and ratios derived from balance sheet accounts. There are often references to the Current Ratio and Working Capital in popular "How-to-Invest" books:

$$\text{Current Ratio} = \frac{\text{Current Assets}}{\text{Current Liabilities}} \qquad (2.1)$$

$$\text{Working Capital} = \text{Current Assets} - \text{Current Liabilities} \qquad (2.2)$$

The authors say the higher the Current Ratio and Working Capital are the better, because that means the company has sufficient liquid assets to meet its current liabilities. The rule of thumb for the Current Ratio is often stipulated at two to one. A Current Ratio higher than two to one is supposed to be good and anything lower is viewed as a cause for concern. Any lender knows relying on the Current Ratio and Working Capital as liquidity proxies is very risky. If a material portion of the receivables are past due more than 90 days or if a chunk of inventory has not been sold for several years, the Current Ratio will overstate the company's liquidity. Furthermore, as long as the levels of the receivables, inventory, and payables are consistent with sound business practice, investors should prefer a *lower* Working Capital number. The less capital is tied up in operating the company, the more cash is available for more productive corporate uses and for dividends and stock buybacks.

FIXED ASSETS AND DEPRECIATION

The plant, property, and equipment account balances in the balance sheet have little utility in an equity analysis. Investors are interested in the expected cash flows generated by the fixed assets of a going concern, not in the book value of fixed assets. The liquidation value of fixed assets is likely to be very different from their book value. Note: A company's annual Depreciation number does *not* tell us how much the company should spend to replace worn-out assets. That is one of the Street's biggest myths. An asset's annual Depreciation expense is its purchase cost divided by management's estimate of the number of years the asset contributes to Revenues.

LEVERAGE AND DEBT SERVICE

The balance sheet provides the balances of the company's debt obligations. The Cash Flow Statement gives the amount by which the debt balance changed from period to period. These are interesting facts, but not nearly as important as how much debt falls due in each year following the balance sheet date and how much cash flow the company generates to service each year's maturing debt. Unless there is little or no debt, there is no such thing as a "strong" balance sheet. The relationship between each future year's debt service requirements (interest plus scheduled principal repayments) and expected cash flow is what counts. To get a company's annual debt service obligation, go to the Notes and look at the debt maturity schedule. It reveals how much debt matures in each of the next five years and then lumps all amounts due in year six and beyond into one number. Unlike the Statement of Cash Flows' financing section, the debt maturity schedule in the Notes is complete because the FASB has included capital leases in the debt maturity schedule. If a company has operating lease payments, those numbers are in the Notes and if material can be included in the calculation of an annual "debt service" number.

WHOSE RETURN ON EQUITY?

Most "How-to-invest" books recommend Return on Equity as a good measurement of financial performance. They define *Return on Equity* as:

$$\text{Return on Equity} = \frac{\text{Annual Net Income}}{\text{Shareholders' Equity}} \tag{2.3}$$

The use of the word *return* in this ratio is egregiously misguided. *Whose* return does this ratio supposedly capture? Certainly a *company's* return on its investments is nowhere to be found in its Return on Equity ratio. Except for stock shares used to make acquisitions, corporate investments are made with cash and return results are measured by cash flow. Whatever Net Income and Shareholders' Equity are, they are not cash numbers. How can

Return on Equity, by any stretch of the imagination, be related to *investor* return? We have already pointed out investor return is not a function of Net Income, book values, or accounting estimates. Investor return is a function of the net difference between cash invested and cash received from the investment. Net Income is an accountant's hypothetical construct. The Retained Earnings account, often the account with the largest balance in Shareholders' Equity, is essentially an aggregate of the current year's Net Income (or Loss) and all prior years' Net Income (or Loss) numbers. So Return on Equity has nothing to do with *return*, at least not for investors and companies. Let's rename the numerator and denominator of the Return on Equity ratio to make them more reflective of reality.

$$\frac{\text{Current Year's Accounting Income (Loss)}}{\text{Stock Par Value} + \text{Paid-in Capital} + \text{Prior Years' Net Income (Loss)}} = ?$$

$$(2.4)$$

What is an appropriate label for "?"? Your guess is as good as mine.

THE NOTES

The Notes provide critical information to investors. Inventory composition, debt schedule, lease schedule, tax, and foreign exchange data as well as business segment data are some of the areas covered in the Notes. Investors must also know whether a company has unfunded pension liabilities and if so, how large they are compared to the company's expected cash flow. If a company is potentially liable for legal penalties, fines, or judgments, investors want to know if the company has sufficient resources to satisfy unfavorable outcomes. The Notes' contribution to investors' understanding of a company cannot be overemphasized.

WHEN DO ACCRUALS MEET CASH FLOWS?

Many investors think all the accruals and cash flows "even out in the end." A viable company has no "end." Every company is continually booking new accruals and modifying existing accruals and reserves. Even if there were no new accrual accounts put on the books, the world in which a company is operating is always changing as is the company itself, so the company must continually reassess and modify its accrual assumptions.

What if a company goes out of business? Will accruals and cash finally coincide? No, because in liquidation the accrual mirage is fully revealed for what it is not. The accruals and shareholders' equity balance are flushed down the drain. All that is left is whatever cash can be generated by the sale of assets. But before the owners get a dollar of the sales' proceeds, taxes and creditors must be paid. The company's owners know one thing for sure: The amount of cash they end up with will not equal the shareholders' equity number on the balance sheet. The owners learn that in the end, only cash counts.

WHAT IS TO BE DONE?

Since public company financial statements are required to follow GAAP, and GAAP is based on accrual accounting, and accrual accounting hides the cash flow as best it can, what are investors to do? Investors must see through the accounting fog by using a financial metric that serves investors' interests. Chapter 3 provides a closer look at Free Cash Flow: how it's different from GAAP Net Income, how it serves investor's interests, and who uses it and why.

CHAPTER 3

Free Cash Flow

Because GAAP accounting hides cash flow under a fog of accruals and allocations, we need to see through the fog to understand what is happening to cash flow and investor return. Free Cash Flow helps us see through much if not all of the fog created by accrual accounting. In this chapter, we first show how we get from Net Income to Free Cash Flow. Then we discuss some of the advantages for investors that Free Cash Flow has over Net Income. Finally, we list some investor groups that use Free Cash Flow and explain why they use it.

RECONCILIATION OF NET INCOME AND FREE CASH FLOW

Our reconciliation is a big picture view of the difference between Net Income and Free Cash Flow. In later chapters we explain Free Cash Flow in greater detail. Exhibit 3.1 has three sections. Section I is a GAAP income statement for a company with Revenues of $100 million and Net Income of $6 million. In Section II, we make adjustments to the GAAP income statement to *remove* noncash expenses *included* in the calculation of GAAP Net Income as well as *add* cash payments that were made by the company but were *excluded* from Net Income. Because Operating Cash Flow is only a partial picture of a company's cash flow chain, in Section III we include both the net *change* in the major Working Capital accounts (accounts receivable, inventory, and accounts payable) and capital expenditures as well as asset sales.

In Section II, we are adding to Net Income the items such as depreciation that reduce Net Income but do not involve cash payments by the company (the company made the cash payments when it purchased the equipment that is being depreciated). After we take out of Net Income such noncash items and return whatever cash items were excluded from the Income Statement, we arrive at Operating Cash Flow. Operating Cash Flow is

EXHIBIT 3.1 Reconciliation of Net Income and Free Cash Flow (000's)

Section I: GAAP Income Statement

Revenues	$100,000
Cost of Sales	−70,000
Gross Profit	30,000
Selling	−3,000
G&A	−15,000
R&D	−2,000
Total Operating Expenses	−20,000
Operating Income	10,000
Interest Expense	−2,000
Pre-tax Income	8,000
Income Tax	−2,000
Net Income	6,000

Section II: GAAP Net Income Is Converted to Operating Cash Flow

Add noncash expenses incorporated in GAAP net income

Depreciation	5,000
Product warranty accrual	3,000
Other non-cash expenses	2,000
Sub-total	10,000

Subtract cash payments not expensed in GAAP income statement

Warranty costs incurred	−2,000
Other cash payments	−1,000
Subtotal	−3,000
Operating Cash Flow	13,000

Section III: Reflects Cash Impact of Working Capital Changes and Capex

Increase in Inventory	−3,000
Decrease in Receivables	2,000
Decrease in Accts. Payable	−1,000
Change in Working Capital	−2,000
Equipment Purchases	−2,000
Computer Purchases	−2,000
Sale of Vehicles	1,000
Total Capex	−3,000
Free Cash Flow	$8,000

what is left after we subtract from Revenues all the costs of operating a business—salaries, wages, benefits, rent, utilities, raw materials, supplies, travel and entertainment, interest on loans, property taxes, payroll taxes, and income taxes. After calculating Operating Cash Flow, we must next incorporate the changes in the company's use of capital. Only the *change* in Working Capital from period to period affects a company's cash flow. When Working Capital increases from one period to the next, cash is consumed by Working Capital. When Working Capital declines, cash is generated. Net Income does not reflect the change in Working Capital. Free Cash Flow incorporates the change in Working Capital. Net Income does not reflect actual Capex. Net Income only reflects the assumptions in the depreciation expense. Free Cash Flow reflects actual Capex.

FREE CASH FLOW VERSUS NET INCOME

How does Free Cash Flow address the problems inherent in GAAP accounting that were listed in Chapter 2? Let's go through them one by one.

1. GAAP: Competing Theories, Matters of Opinion, Political Compromises

   By eliminating the credits and charges in Net Income that are enumerated in the GAAP Cash Flow Statement, we have reduced but not eliminated the impact of the *theories, opinion,* and *compromises.*

2. GAAP Accrual Abuse

   Free Cash Flow investors are less vulnerable to accrual abuse than Earnings Per Share (EPS) investors, but all investors are always vulnerable to distortions, exaggerations, and omissions made by management.

3. GAAP: Errors Bred by Complexity

   Free Cash Flow investors are also vulnerable to unintentional management accounting errors.

4. GAAP's Gap

   Free Cash Flow investors have an advantage over EPS investors to the extent that differences between GAAP earnings and cash flows suggest accounting fraud may be occurring.

5. GAAP EPS: An Incomplete Definition of Financial Performance

   EPS includes accounting estimates, excludes working capital changes, and substitutes Depreciation expense for Capex. Free Cash Flow excludes most accounting estimates, includes Working Capital changes, and uses actual Capex instead of Depreciation. Because Free Cash Flow is a cash-based metric, the investor can use Free Cash Flow (but *not* Net Income) as the starting point for an analysis of a company's deployment of cash—for acquisitions, stock buybacks, dividends, and debt repayments. Because Free Cash Flow is a cash-based metric, the investor can integrate a company's creation and deployment of Free Cash Flow in a comprehensive analysis of investor return.

6. GAAP EPS: Investing in an Economic Vacuum

   EPS is a noncash (actually an anticash) metric. Investors seek cash returns. Free Cash Flow enables investors to assess a company's financial performance and prospects, per item 5 above, and then to compare the potential return from an investment in the company to the potential returns from investing in alternative investments.

A UNIVERSAL DEFINITION?

There is no generally accepted definition of Free Cash Flow. Some investors exclude changes in Working Capital from the definition. Some analysts estimate maintenance Capex (how much Capex is allocated to maintaining existing equipment and other fixed assets) and include only maintenance Capex in Free Cash Flow. Separating maintenance Capex and new Capex is in theory a good idea but in practice usually unworkable because most companies do not disclose the breakdown of Capex dollars into maintenance of existing assets and purchase of new assets. Our Capex is the Capex in the GAAP Cash Flow plus any new assets financed by capital leases.

Many public companies include a pro forma definition of Free Cash Flow toward the end of their quarterly earnings press releases. The vast majority use the same two numbers from the GAAP Statement of Cash Flow. They define Free Cash Flow as the "Cash provided by operating activities" line minus the capital expenditures number in the Investing section. This definition of Free Cash Flow results in the same Free Cash Flow number we use. Do *not* infer, however, that because a company includes a Free Cash Flow calculation in its press releases, that means management is managing to Free Cash Flow. Press releases mention Free Cash Flow because the CFOs of these companies realize Free Cash Flow is important to sell-side analysts and large institutional investors. The CFO is trying to send a signal to the Street that the company also considers Free Cash Flow to be an important financial metric. For most companies, however, the pro forma Free Cash Flow in the press release is nothing more than a PR stunt. Most managers' bonuses are based on the company's EPS, so the company is managed to EPS. In Chapter 8, we will discuss what motivates the CEO.

ACADEMIC RESEARCH AND THE DISCOUNTED CASH FLOW MODEL

A good deal of academic research on public company valuation has concluded that a company's stock price is determined by the stock market's assessment of the company's expected cash flows, not by the company's historical or expected GAAP earnings. GAAP EPS as a valuation tool has long been discredited. Dr. Alfred Rappaport, Professor Emeritus of Northwestern University, is the author of *Creating Shareholder Value: A Guide for Managers and Investors,* a leading book on financial management. Professor Rappaport explains that expected cash flows, rather than GAAP earnings, is the primary determinant of stock prices. He also points out that public company announcements regarding changes in accounting methods do not affect stock prices unless there are also changes in expected cash flows.[1]

McKinsey & Company's Tim Koller, Marc Goedhart, and David Wessels are the authors of one of the pre-eminent studies on corporate finance and equity valuation: *Valuation: Measuring and Managing the Value of Companies.* They conclude: "Share prices are determined by long-term cash flows."[2] The authors also show that earnings announcements affect stock prices only when the news suggests long-term cash flows will be affected. Changes in accounting practices that do not affect long-term cash flows do not affect stock prices. According to Koller, Goedhart, and Wessels, "The market is not interested in accounting choices; investors care about underlying performance."[3]

If expected cash flows drive stock prices, why do sell-side analysts talk so much about EPS? Public companies are required by the SEC to use GAAP in disclosing their financial results. This government requirement sets the metric table, so to speak, for market participants and commentators. The business schools did not get into valuation research until the 1960s or so. Also, while sell-side analysts communicate their target prices based on the simplistic language of the Street—EPS and PE multiples—many analysts use Discounted Cash Flow (DCF) valuation models to derive their valuations.

A DCF model begins innocently enough with a 10-year projection of Free Cash Flow. But right after the Free Cash Flow projection, things get highly hypothetical. The analyst chooses a discount rate to discount the projected annual Free Cash Flow numbers. The choice of a discount rate is more art than science. Then, the present value of the discounted Free Cash Flows is added to the *terminal value* of the company. The terminal value is the analyst's estimate of the total value of the company's Free Cash Flows *beyond* the 10-year projection period. Each sell-side analyst covering a company, therefore, has unique Free Cash Flow projections, discount rates, and terminal values supporting the stock valuations. The Free Cash Flow Statement and the Free Cash Flow Worksheet provide the investor with the necessary tools to use Free Cash Flow as a primary metric without having to speculate about discount rates and terminal values.

BARRON'S RANKINGS

Barron's newspaper periodically publishes a ranking of the stock-picking records of the major brokers. In an interview in November 2006 with Greg Forsythe, the creator of Schwab's stock-picking model, *Barron's* says that since 2003 Schwab "...dominated the long-term rankings compiled by Zacks Investment Research, which compares the focus lists of about a dozen major Wall Street brokerages. Schwab has been first in either the three- or five-year period in each ranking, except one, when it finished second over three years."[4] According to *Barron's*, Schwab uses 18 variables in the Schwab Equity Ratings (SER) model and Free Cash Flow is "'...very, very important,' the biggest single driver behind the SER ratings...."[5] Schwab's definition of Free Cash Flow is "...net income plus depreciation and minus capital expenditures and dividends...."[6] So Schwab's Free Cash Flow definition differs from our definition because they exclude Working Capital changes and the other items in the Operating section of the GAAP Cash Flow, and they include dividends.

In a subsequent brokerage firm rating article, *Barron's* reported that Schwab was no longer ranked number one for the six-month and one-year periods.[7] There was a new champ in the six-month and one-year categories: Matrix USA. Morgan Keegan was in first place for the three-year period. Goldman Sachs and Schwab were essentially tied for first place for five years with Smith Barney coming in a close third. *Barron's* says, "High among Matrix's considered factors are excess Free Cash Flow and excess cash per share.... Unlike many rivals, 'We don't use analyst Earnings-Per-Share estimates.'"[8] Let's go to the five-year rankings. Here is *Barron's* explanation as to why Smith Barney's investment approach was so successful: "...[O]ver those five years, its (Smith Barney's) focus on Free Cash Flow and profit margins led to a selection of stocks that happen to be sectors in demand by investors, helping to produce the nearly 108% return...."[9] To be sure, we do not know precisely how each of the winning brokerage firms defines Free

Cash Flow. And even if they provided a definition, we would have to assume the definition is subjected to various tweaks as the analysts move through their modeling process. Nor, unfortunately, can we conclude the winning brokers won *because* they used Free Cash Flow as a primary analytical metric. Investing involves way too many variables to do that. But it appears that Free Cash Flow is used by some of the most successful stock pickers.

BUY-SIDE USERS

Stock prices are driven primarily by the large financial institutions: the mutual funds, insurance companies, banks, and investment management firms. Many of these professional investors employ Free Cash Flow as an important tool in their investment decisions. A number of major investment management firms use sophisticated software to circumvent the problems with GAAP accounting. This software strips away the GAAP accruals in public company financial statements so they can calculate Free Cash Flow. These large firms are not investing in special software just to eliminate the impact of the depreciation expense on earnings per share! They have concluded the aggregate impact of the many noncash items in the GAAP income statement materially distorts the financial results of public companies. Wall Street firms are convinced they can make money for themselves and their clients by seeing through the GAAP accounting fog.

PRIVATE EQUITY FIRMS

Private equity firms and hedge funds use Free Cash Flow models when they evaluate potential equity investments. They have learned, sometimes the hard way, that GAAP numbers are problematic at best and misleading at worst. They use Free Cash Flow because that is the best way to evaluate the potential of an investment to produce the required investment return. Also, these investors frequently use debt to acquire complete or partial ownership of a company. A company's ability to generate Free Cash Flow to repay the debt is an important part of the due diligence analysis conducted by private equity firms.

WARREN WHO?

Very few private equity outfits have Warren Buffett's long and successful investment track record. Does he use GAAP EPS or cash flow? Warren

Buffett uses cash flow to value companies he's interested in buying. Here's a passage from Robert G. Hagstrom Jr.'s *The Essential Buffett: Timeless Principles for the New Economy:*

"Through the years, financial analysts have used many formulas for calculating the intrinsic value of a company. Some are fond of various shorthand methods: low price-to-earnings ratios, low price-to-book values, and high dividend yields. But the best system, according to Buffett, was determined more than 60 years ago by John Burr Williams in *The Theory of Investment Value.* Paraphrasing Williams' theory, Buffett tells us the value of a business is the total of the net cash flows (owners' earnings) expected to occur over the life of the business, discounted by an appropriate interest rate."[10]

A VAST MEDIA CONSPIRACY?

The financial media are always talking about EPS as the primary driver of stock prices. Is there some conspiracy between the financial media and Wall Street to hide Free Cash Flow? Not at all. True, financial news anchors usually do not mention Free Cash Flow but their guests—the sell-side analysts and buy-side portfolio managers—often do in explaining why they like specific stocks. Or take *Barron's* interviews with investment managers and analysts. A significant number of portfolio managers and analysts interviewed in *Barron's* cite Free Cash Flow as one of their primary stock-picking criteria. So, it depends on where we look and whom we listen to. In any event, we want to use what we understand and what works, whether or not it is part of the media lexicon. As a matter of fact, even the staff of the FASB has provided information on the relative value to Street analysts of Net Income versus Free Cash Flow.

FASB STAFF FINDINGS

In 2002, the Financial Accounting Standards Board (FASB) staff presented to its Board the results of field research on the use of public company financial statements. The staff had interviewed some 56 users of financial statements, including 32 sell-side analysts and 9 buy-side analysts and portfolio managers. The FASB staff concluded that "Most analysts interviewed focus primarily on operating cash flow/Free Cash Flow or operating earnings."[11] The staff also found that "GAAP net income is not the focus for most users' assessments of company performance."[12] The FASB staff said Net Income is not "... generally among the three most important measures."[13]

FAS 95: A CRUEL RULE

We've talked about quarterly earnings press releases and noted many of them include a pro forma Free Cash Flow calculation. But there has never been a Free Cash Flow *per share* number in the quarterly earnings release of a U.S. public company. Why not? Because it is *forbidden*. In FAS 95, the FASB prohibits Free Cash Flow per share from appearing in financial statements prepared in accordance with Generally Accepted Accounting Principles. That means if a public company wanted to include its Free Cash Flow per share numbers in its financial statements, the company could not receive a clean opinion from its outside auditors. Why would the FASB take the trouble to prohibit a Free Cash Flow per share number from appearing in public company financial disclosures? Here's one guess: The SEC and the FASB believe American investors are not smart enough to use Free Cash Flow per share. The SEC and FASB have concocted Earnings Per Share—the Government Number—to protect investors from being confused by fluctuations in cash flow. They are convinced investors would become disoriented and delirious if we tried to use Free Cash Flow per share in our investment analysis. So the SEC and FASB slam the door on Free Cash Flow per share.

EPS MISSES: THE REAL DEAL

Every quarter a number of companies miss their quarterly EPS targets by a few cents and immediately their stocks get clobbered, dropping by 10 percent or 15 percent and sometimes more. Some investors think this shows how important EPS is to a company's stock price. As a matter of fact, it shows just the opposite. Say the quarter's EPS target was $1.00. A company missing the $1.00 target by two cents missed by 2 percent. It is unlikely the stock dropped 10 percent or 20 percent in one day simply because the company missed its EPS target by 2 percent. If that were the case, it would imply that the market is composed of investors who trash their investments because an EPS target is missed by a immaterial amount. Stock prices are not driven by a company's ability to meet its EPS target to the penny but rather by the company's prospects for the future. If the stock dropped 20 percent on a 2 percent EPS miss, the drop was probably due to some combination of the following reasons: (1) actual Free Cash Flow for the quarter just announced was lower than the anticipated Free Cash Flow to an extent that subsequent Free Cash Flow per share performance has been called into question; or (2) management guidance and comments in the press release or in the subsequent conference call resulted in a downward revision of the market's expectations for Free Cash Flow per share.

AN ALTERNATIVE TO THE GOVERNMENT NUMBER

The SEC has delegated to the FASB the authority to promulgate the accounting rules that must be followed by public companies. That makes EPS a Government Number. The alternative to the Government Number is Free Cash Flow per share. Unlike GAAP EPS, Free Cash Flow per share captures Revenues, *Cash* Margin, *and* use of Capital. We will build the Free Cash Flow Statement in the next chapter.

CHAPTER 4

The Free Cash Flow Statement

I n Chapter 3 we showed how Free Cash Flow is derived from Net Income. We are now going to put aside Net Income and EPS and build the Free Cash Flow Statement. The Free Cash Flow Statement has some unique advantages over both the GAAP Income Statement as well as conventional Free Cash Flow definitions.

BUILDING THE FREE CASH FLOW STATEMENT

Step 1: Revenues

To build the Free Cash Flow Statement, we first go the company's Income Statement to get the Revenues number. We will assume our hypothetical public company, ABC Corporation, had Revenues of $500 million in 2006. All numbers are in thousands.

ABC Corporation Free Cash Flow Statement	2006
Revenues	$500,000

The only other number we will need from the Income Statement is the average number of common shares outstanding in 2006. ABC had 20 million shares. Everything else needed to make our Free Cash Flow Statement is in Exhibit 4.1: ABC's GAAP Cash Flow Statement.

Step 2: Calculate Operating Cash Flow

Our objective in Step 2 is to get as close as we can to an Operating Cash Flow number that incorporates the Cash Operating Costs definition of the furniture company in Chapter 1: "Uses cash to pay its operating costs such as employee salaries, wages and benefits, suppliers, utility bills, legal and

EXHIBIT 4.1 ABC's Consolidated Statements of Cash Flows

1	**Operating Activities**	**2006**
2	Net Income	$78,000
3	Charges and credits:	
4	Depreciation and amortization	6,500
5	Warranty costs incurred	(120)
6	Share-based compensation expense	90
7	Gain on sale of Chicago plant	(9,500)
8	Other	(2,000)
9	Changes in working capital items:	
10	Accounts receivable	(3,000)
11	Inventories	(6,000)
12	Accounts payable	5,000
13	Other	(1,000)
14	Net working capital items	(5,000)
15	Net cash provided by operating activities	67,970
16	**Investing activities**	
17	Property and equipment expenditures	(19,500)
18	Sale of equipment	250
19	Sale of Chicago plant	2,475
20	Net cash used for investing activities	(16,775)
21	**Financing activities**	
22	Proceeds from long term debt	5,000
23	Repayments of long term debt	(10,000)
24	Treasury stock purchases	(8,000)
25	Common stock dividends	(3,000)
26	Proceeds from stock option exercises	500
27	Net cash used for financing activities	(15,500)
28	**Cash and equivalents increase/(decrease)**	35,695
29	Cash and equivalents at beginning of year	12,500
30	Cash and equivalents at end of year	$48,195
31	**Supplemental cash flow disclosures**	
32	Interest paid	$1,000
33	Income taxes paid	2,500

accounting fees, taxes, interest on debt if any, and so forth...." Changes in balance sheet accounts, however, are not direct cash costs but rather continually fluctuating sources and uses of cash. Take inventories as an example. An increase in the inventories balance is a use of cash. This use of cash does not directly add to the company's product costs. To the extent a build-up in inventories results in incremental financing costs, storage costs, or insurance costs, *only* these incremental cash costs—*not* the change in the balance of the inventories account—are included in the company's Cash Operating Costs.

Before we introduce our Operating Cash Flow formula, let's look at the top section (Lines 1–15) of the GAAP Cash Flow. This top section is called "Cash provided by operating activities," or "Operating Activities" or "Cash from operations," or something similar. We will use "CFO section" as our shorthand for the top section. "Net CFO" is our shorthand for the "Net cash provided by operating activities" number on Line 15 of the CFO section. The CFO section always starts at the top with Net Income (or Net Loss). To get from Net Income to Net CFO, the GAAP Cash Flow makes two types of adjustments to the Net Income number:

- Type 1: All of the *noncash* items included in the Net Income number are *removed* from Net Income.
- Type 2: All of the *cash* items *not* included in the Net Income number are added to or subtracted from Net Income.

Directly below Net Income in Lines 3–8 are the various "Charges and credits" to Net Income. Both Type 1 and Type 2 items are found in the Charges and credits group. The $6.5 million Depreciation and amortization number on Line 4 is a Type 1 adjustment. Depreciation is a noncash charge included in the calculation of Net Income, so it was added back to Net Income. Another Type 1 item is the "Gain on sale of the Chicago plant" on Line 7. This is an accounting or *book* gain, not a cash gain, so the $9.5 million was removed by subtracting it from Net Income. "Warranty costs incurred" on Line 5 is an example of a Type 2 adjustment. ABC used $120,000 in cash to satisfy customer claims against product warranties. The $120,000 cash expenditure was absorbed by the company's warranty reserve rather than being charged against income. If the warranty reserve is replenished by a noncash charge to Income, that noncash item is either listed separately in the Charges and credits group or it is included in the group's "Other" on Line 8.

The changes in ABC's Working Capital accounts are grouped together at the bottom of the CFO section in Lines 9–14. Many companies also include the changes in noncurrent asset and liabilities accounts. We frequently use the delta symbol ("Δ") to mean "change(s) in." We use "Δ Working Capital" as our shorthand label for *all the balance sheet changes*—both current and noncurrent—grouped together at the bottom of the CFO section.

To calculate our unique definition of Operating Cash Flow, we remove from Net CFO all of the balance sheet changes listed in the CFO.

$$\text{Operating Cash Flow} = \text{Net CFO} +/- \Delta\text{WC}$$
$$= \$67,970 + \$5,000$$
$$= \$72,970 \qquad (4.1)$$

ABC's $67,970 of Net CFO *includes* the ($5,000) net use of cash for Working Capital accounts. Because we want our Operating Cash Flow number to equal Net CFO *before* the GAAP Cash Flow's balance sheet adjustments, we must *add* the $5,000 back to the $67,970 number. In ABC's case, the $72,970 number is Net Income *after* the *nonbalance sheet* charges and credits but *before* the GAAP Cash Flow's balance sheet adjustments. What does this accomplish? By removing the balance sheet changes from Net CFO, we get an Operating Cash Flow number that is a net of Revenues and cash costs *without* the distortions created by the balance sheet changes. This is not to say balance sheet changes are unimportant. But rather than bury them in the Net CFO number, we explicitly incorporate them in Step 5 of the Free Cash Flow Statement.

Note: Our Operating Cash Flow formula differs from the most common use of this term. *Operating Cash Flow* is used on the Street as a synonym for Net CFO (Line 15). Net CFO *includes* the balance sheet changes while our definition *excludes* balance sheet changes.

Step 3: Calculate Cash Operating Costs

Having derived Operating Cash Flow, we can now bring in Revenues and calculate the difference between ABC's Revenues and its Operating Cash Flow. The difference is Cash Operating Costs.

$$\text{Cash Op. Costs} = \text{Revenues} - \text{Op. Cash Flow}$$
$$= \$500,000 - \$72,970$$
$$= \$427,030 \qquad (4.2)$$

Now we have the first three lines of the Free Cash Flow Statement.

ABC Corporation

Free Cash Flow Statement	2006
Revenues	$500,000
− Cash Operating Costs	427,030
= Operating Cash Flow	72,970

Step 4: Calculate Operating Cash Flow Margin

We can now capture the company's Operating Cash Flow Margin because we have removed the balance sheet changes.

$$\text{Operating Cash Flow Margin} = \frac{\text{Operating Cash Flow}}{\text{Revenues}}$$
$$= \frac{\$72,790}{\$500,000} = 15\% \qquad (4.3)$$

The Free Cash Flow Statement is the *only* format that includes a cash cost margin. Comparing companies without a cash cost margin is like piloting a plane in the clouds without instruments.

Step 5: Calculate Δ Working Capital

Recall that ABC's GAAP Cash Flow includes the calculation of the ($5,000) net use of cash for the Working Capital accounts. Recall in Step 2 we added the $5,000 net use of cash back to the $67,970 Net CFO number to get to our $72,970 Operating Cash Flow number. Now, because we want Free Cash Flow to incorporate the Δ Working Capital number, we will subtract the Δ Working Capital number if it is a negative number (negative numbers are uses of cash) and add the Δ Working Capital number if it is a positive number (positive numbers are sources of cash). Because ABC's Δ Working Capital is a *negative* $5,000 (a use of cash), we subtract $5,000 from Operating Cash Flow.

ABC Corporation Free Cash Flow Statement	2006
Revenues	$500,000
− Cash Operating Costs	427,030
= Operating Cash Flow	72,970
− Δ Working Capital	5,000

Step 6: Capex

ABC's Capex is on Line 17 in the Investing section and is $19,500. To be consistent with the Free Cash Flow Worksheet, we are ignoring all negative parentheses in the GAAP Cash Flow after we leave the Working Capital section of the CFO.

ABC Corporation

Free Cash Flow Statement	2006
Revenues	$500,000
− Cash Operating Costs	427,030
= Operating Cash Flow	72,970
− Δ Working Capital	5,000
− Capex	19,500

Step 7: Free Cash Flow

Here is the first look at the entire Free Cash Flow Statement:

ABC Corporation

Free Cash Flow Statement	2006
Revenues	$500,000
− Cash Operating Costs	427,030
= Operating Cash Flow	72,970
− Δ Working Capital	5,000
− Capex	19,500
= Free Cash Flow	$48,470

Step 8: Calculate Free Cash Flow per Share (FCS)

We are focused on our share of the firm's Free Cash Flow, so we convert the Free Cash Flow number to a per share number.

$$\text{Free Cash Flow per share (FCS)} = \frac{\text{Free CashFlow}}{\text{Number of Shares}}$$

$$= \frac{\$48,470}{20,000} = \$2.42 \qquad (4.4)$$

Remember what FCS means. *We will use it a lot.*

FOUR KEY QUESTIONS

The Free Cash Flow Statement addresses four key questions:

1. What is happening to *Revenues?*
2. What is happening to the cash costs' *Margin?*

3. What is happening to *Capital* utilization?
4. What is happening to Free Cash Flow?

The GAAP Net Income Statement addresses question 1. Net Income does not answer question 2 because Net Income is materially affected by accrual allocations. Net Income is silent on the Working Capital component of question 3 because the Net Income Statement ignores Working Capital changes. The Capex portion of a company's capital utilization is not accurately reflected in Net Income to the extent Capex differs materially from the Depreciation expense.

Except for the DCF model, the most common Street definition of Free Cash Flow is:

ABC Corporation
Street Free Cash Flow

Net CFO	$67,970
− Capex	19,500
= Free Cash Flow	$48,470

The Free Cash Flow Statement and the Street definition of Free Cash Flow both result in the same Free Cash Flow number for ABC: $48,470. The Street formula, however, ignores Revenues and the cash operating margin. Capex is broken out in the Street formula but Δ Working Capital is embedded in the Net CFO number rather than broken out as it is in the Free Cash Flow Statement.

In sum, *only the Free Cash Flow Statement answers all four questions.* Now let's go through each of the components of the Free Cash Flow Statement.

REVENUES

Revenues are the prerequisite for Free Cash Flow, but the Free Cash Flow investor approaches Revenues with a cold, objective attitude. Many EPS investors mistakenly chase rapidly rising Revenues that generate higher EPS but reduce Free Cash Flow. In the Free Cash Flow Statement, we break out the Working Capital and Capex used to generate the Revenues. Unfortunately, all too often companies produce terrific Revenue growth rates while sacrificing margins and/or using excessive amounts of capital. Revenue jumps that initially appear to be investor-friendly because they are GAAP-profitable may turn out to require large, continuous infusions of capital for Capex. If Capex is so large that it continuously results in negative Free Cash

Flow—year after year—then the company is not likely to be a source of attractive long-term investor returns.

Always consider the two major factors that determine a company's Revenues: unit volumes and unit prices. To be sure, this is easier for some industries than for others. For competitive reasons, companies often do not disclose much useful information about volumes and prices. Nonetheless, it is useful to subject each Revenue number to this basic question: How much of the change in Revenues from the prior period was a result of volume changes and how much was a result of price changes? Management is often asked about this in the quarterly conference call. A large Revenue increase that reflects a sacrifice of prices for higher volumes may not be repeatable on a long-term basis. It may also result in lower margins and higher Working Capital, especially if management granted very lenient credit terms to stimulate Revenues. Revenue growth that reduces Free Cash Flow may well be necessary to generate higher long-term returns for investors. But a company that chronically produces Revenue increases and negative Free Cash Flows does not include investor return among its priorities.

Always understand a company's dependence on its major products/services and its major customers. The smaller the company, the more important are its product and customer concentrations. Many small cap companies started out with one product and several large customers. A lot of these firms have grown over the years and now appear to have a large variety of products and numerous customers. But below the surface, many small cap companies remain significantly dependent on one or two products and several customers for a large chunk of their Revenues and Free Cash Flow. Customer concentration data is provided in the 10-Qs and 10-K.

Investors must always be on the lookout for the CEO who is essentially nothing more than a Chief Revenue Officer. Of course the CEO must be the Chief Revenue Officer, but the CEO must also be the Chief Margin Officer and the Chief Capital Officer. The Chief Margin Officer knows how to price products and services and manage costs so that the company generates a strong, sustainable Operating Cash Flow Margin. The Chief Capital Officer must manage capital utilization so the company's investors earn an attractive return on their investment. Most CEOs spent most of their formative years in sales and marketing jobs. Increasing Revenues was not just an important goal for these future CEOs—it was *the* goal. Generating large sales increases is how they got the largest bonuses and their promotions. The promotion to the CEO job leads to broader responsibilities than those of a Vice President-Sales but the promotion does not necessarily change mindset and priorities. Many CEOs believe if sales can be increased, then profits will somehow follow.

The determination of Revenues incorporates many assumptions made by management. Not all companies in the same industry recognize Revenue in the same way. Some oil and gas companies, for example, recognize Revenues only when the customer approves the completed project while other oil and gas companies recognize Revenue over the course of the project. Free Cash Flow does not enable the investor to evade all of the countless estimates that go into preparing financial statements. Keep this in mind when using the Operating Cash Flow Margin.

OPERATING CASH FLOW

Operating Cash Flow is critical because it gives us the Operating Cash Flow Margin, a very useful tool in our analysis of historical statements and our projection of a company's Free Cash Flow. Again, ABC Corporation's operating cash flow margin is:

$$\text{Operating Cash Flow Margin} = \frac{\text{Operating Cash Flow}}{\text{Revenues}}$$

$$= \frac{\$72,790}{\$500,000} = 15\% \qquad (4.3)$$

The Operating Cash Flow Margin provides a crucial perspective on a company's long-term cost trends. Because Operating Cash Flow includes no accruals, it is relatively free of the estimates and guesstimates of the accountants. Do we gain more than we lose by focusing on Operating Cash Flow rather than on the major expense items in the GAAP Income Statement? Gross Profit Margin includes Depreciation and other production-related noncash expenses. How many stocks are we going to buy or sell because of the SG&A numbers? For some industries like drugs and technology, R&D is significant and crucial to a company's success. However, unless an investor has specific-industry expertise, it may be difficult to know how to interpret R&D trends. The Free Cash Flow investor can use Income Statement and other GAAP data when appropriate to augment the Free Cash Flow analysis without losing focus on the fundamental sources of return.

The Operating Cash Flow Margin is a revealing window into how efficiently the company is managed compared to its competitors. That is because Operating Cash Flow is not clouded up by the companies' differing accruals and estimates. A peer group comparison with several years of Operating Cash Flow Margins should provide some insight into management's effectiveness. If other companies in the industry are enjoying consistently higher or increasing Operating Cash Flow Margins, it is probably a good idea to move on to the next stock unless there are solid reasons to expect a material improvement.

Which is better for investors: Revenue growth or an increase in Operating Cash Flow Margin? Both are better, of course, but there can be a difference between the two in regard to their impact on Free Cash Flow. If a company requires a relatively large amount of capital to generate additional sales, the benefit to Free Cash Flow will be muted by the required capital investment. If the same company were to focus on increasing the Operating Cash Flow Margin instead of on increasing sales, the entire benefit of the higher Operating Cash Flow Margin would increase Free Cash Flow. This is one example of how focusing on less is more. An EPS mindset does not typically think in terms of the total return on investment chain and often minimizes the impact of capital use on investor returns. The Free Cash Flow Statement is not as detailed as a GAAP Income Statement, but the Free Cash Flow Statement encourages, and in fact requires, the investor to focus on what really counts.

Because the Free Cash Flow Statement consists of cash numbers, not accrual-plus-cash numbers, the Free Cash Flow investor can relate Operating Cash Flow or any of the components of the Free Cash Flow Statement to a company's operational data such as number of stores, number of employees, plant square footage, and so on. Can we do that with GAAP numbers? Those investors who combine GAAP numbers with operational metrics ignore the hypothetical nature of GAAP margins.

Δ WORKING CAPITAL

Changes in Working Capital probably receive less attention from investors than any of the other components of the Free Cash Flow chain. Working Capital is not as concrete and straightforward as Revenues, costs, and Capex. Δ Working Capital is undoubtedly the most difficult Free Cash Flow component to visualize because it has so many moving parts often going in opposite directions. The fact that assets and liabilities are mixed together makes a snapshot interpretation all the more difficult. Analyzing Working Capital is a bit like juggling balls—it must be done frequently to do it well. Let's review how changes in Working Capital accounts affect cash flow.

$$
\begin{array}{ccc}
 & \underline{2006} & \\
+/-\Delta \text{ Working Capital} & (\$5,000) & \quad (4.4)
\end{array}
$$

EXHIBIT 4.2 Working Capital

	Balance as of		Difference
	12/31/06	12/31/05	Source (Use) of Cash
Accounts Receivable	$41,000	$38,000	$(3,000)
Inventory	57,000	51,000	(6,000)
Accounts Payable	44,000	39,000	5,000
Other—Net	18,000	19,000	(1,000)
Net Change			$(5,000)

The $5 million use of cash is the net of the changes in the accounts receivable, inventory, accounts payable, and other working capital (see Exhibit 4.2) items from 12/31/05 to 12/31/06.

Receivables increased $3 million from 12/31/05 to 12/31/06. This increase in receivables *consumed* cash, and that is why the number in the Difference column is a negative $3 million. Another asset, Inventory, increased $6 million, and that is also a use of cash, so the number in the Difference column is also negative. When asset accounts other than Cash and equivalents increase, that is a use of cash and when asset accounts decrease, the decrease is a source of cash. When liability accounts increase, the increase is a source of cash. In the example above, Accounts Payable increased $5 million, so the change in Payables was a source of cash. When liability accounts decrease, that is a use of cash.

The Working Capital section is the one area where management can most easily manipulate the Free Cash Flow number, particularly in one accounting period. Management can delay paying vendor invoices, thereby increasing the Accounts Payable balance. Less likely manipulations are accelerating collections of Accounts Receivable and not replenishing Inventory. Watch days' payables, receivables, and inventory trends to make sure the company is not manipulating Net CFO and Free Cash Flow. Free Cash Flow investors must be especially alert to manipulation of Working Capital balances because management can play these games without the approval of the company's outside auditors.

CAPEX

Capex and investor return are like oil and water. Obviously, some Capex is essential. But investors in companies with large and persistent Capex numbers often receive not much more than the corporate crumbs. Some CEOs enjoy nothing more than buying equipment or buildings or airplanes or whatever. I have worked with hundreds of CEOs and CFOs. They are great managers who are much smarter and more knowledgeable than this author. But many CEOs are clueless when it comes to finance and do not understand how unnecessary Capex (and sometimes necessary Capex) reduces investor returns below acceptable levels. There are seven major types of Capex:

1. Maintenance
2. Productivity enhancement projects
3. Capacity expansion for existing products
4. New capacity for new products
5. IT spending
6. Environmental requirements
7. Ego projects

Maintenance Capex is for necessary equipment rebuilds and similar projects. For example, a paper manufacturer may have to completely rebuild a papermaking machine every six or seven years. These projects can result in large Capex spikes. An ego project is Capex that makes management feel better but results in an unnecessary decrease in Free Cash Flow and investor return.

It is usually not possible to a detailed breakdown of a public company's Capex. But try to determine how the company is allocating its Capex dollars—if only in a very broad-brush way—over a period of several years. Try to find out if the company is spending most of its Capex dollars on (1), (2), (3), or (4). These uses of capital can potentially generate higher long term Free Cash Flows. If, on the other hand, the company appears to be investing much of its Capex in (5), (6), or (7), there are 12,000 other public companies to analyze. This is not a criticism of IT or environmental projects per se, but such projects can be difficult to manage to budget, especially if no one on the management team is experienced in the specific project.

CAPEX: MAGNITUDE AND RISK

Investors must have a sense of the relative size and risk of a company's typical Capex project. Capex for one new restaurant, for example, is a small percentage of a restaurant chain's Operating Cash Flow or Free Cash Flow. On the other hand, one large refinery could account for a large percentage of a medium-sized refiner's Operating Cash Flow. Manufacturing Capex is often more complex, riskier, and takes more time than putting up and fitting out a new restaurant site. Here are some questions to ask about Capex:

- How dependent on Capex is the company for Revenue growth?
- What opportunities does the company have to increase Revenues without major Capex spending?
- How large is the company's typical capacity-increase project relative to annual Revenues? Is the annual Capex mostly $1 million projects or is it more like a $1 billion new plant with new technology?
- How much risk is in the Capex? Capex risk can be divided into three components: budget risk, schedule risk, and performance risk. Does the company have a good track record of completing large projects on budget, on time, and within expected performance specifications? Is an ongoing large Capex program a first-of-its-kind project?
- Is the company spending *enough* on Capex? We do not want to invest in companies that are trying to increase cash flow by ignoring required maintenance and enhancement projects. What are other companies in the industry spending on Capex as a percentage of Revenues?
- Is the company a Capex machine or an investor return machine? *It is possible but difficult to be both.*

For information on a company's Capex, listen to the quarterly conference calls. Read the MD&A and also the Liquidity and Capital Adequacy sections of the 10-Qs and 10-Ks. Look at the press releases. Do a search on the company name and words such as *spending, new facilities, plant,* or other words appropriate for the industry. Also look at the Capex assumptions in analysts' models if sell-side analysts are following the company.

CAPEX AND CAPITAL

Large Capex spending often requires new capital. The more Capex a company needs to support growing Revenues, the more outside financing the company requires to bridge the cash flow timing gap between the purchase of the Capex and the Revenues generated by the Capex. If new equity is raised to fund the Capex, the new shares dilute the existing shareholders. If debt is used, the debt takes priority over shareholders' claims on the company's cash flows and thereby reduces the company's valuation, at least in the short term. Debt also reduces Free Cash Flow because interest must be paid. When Capex investments work out as planned, all parties can often benefit, including management, employees, customers, suppliers, and investors. That should be how firms expand capacity and introduce new products. But frequently investors support management teams who, year after year spend too much on Capex or take excessive risks with their Capex investments. To the extent unnecessary Capex projects are financed by new debt or new equity, investors pay a double price.

CAPEX TRANSFER

Before we leave Capex, let's consider Capex Transfer, an important trend among large companies that benefits Free Cash Flows and investor returns. Major U.S. and other global companies have been outsourcing much of their production facilities to low-cost countries such as China and India. In doing so, these Fortune 1000 companies have been reducing their labor costs and improving their profitability. *Barron's* did a long interview with GaveKal, an investment research firm that has done a lot of work in this area. Motorola, HP, Dell, Caterpillar, and Black & Decker are just a few examples. This trend has been well-publicized because outsourcing has unfortunately resulted in the loss of hundreds of thousands of manufacturing jobs in the United States. What has not been highlighted by the news media is the transfer of Capex from U.S. manufacturers' Free Cash Flows to Chinese and Indian partners or subcontractors. The Free Cash Flows of these global U.S. companies have benefited in two ways: higher Operating Cash Flows because of the reduction in labor costs and lower Capex because of the Capex Transfer. Not surprisingly, these changes have contributed to stronger Free Cash Flows, higher dividends, and lower debt levels, all of which benefit investors. Some of these global companies are investing what were previously Capex dollars into R&D and training.[2] Of course, Capex transferred to foreign companies can always return to the United States. If oil prices or other cost factors make manufacturing outsourcing uneconomic, Capex will rise again, and if it does, Free Cash Flow investors will be the first to see its impact.

CAPEX VISIBILITY

Which is going to show the benefit of a company's Capex Transfer sooner: the company's EPS or its Free Cash Flow per share? Here's a head start on the question: Labor cost savings will not show up all that much differently in EPS and FCS. But in a GAAP Income Statement, the depreciation expense includes the depreciation expenses of both existing equipment and any new Capex acquired in the period. The depreciation expense of the new Capex

Letters

Current accounting fiction that is extemely dangerous

From Mr Paul Phillips.

Sir, Martin Taylor's excellent article "Innumerate bankers were ripe for a reckoning" (December 16) goes straight to the core of one of the main causes of the banking crisis – and moreover one that there seems to be very little appetite to reform.

He makes the point that banks' accounting profits consist, as a result of mark-to-market accounting, to a very significant degree of future payment streams, such as swap payments, stretching in some cases many years into the future. It is not be converted into actual cash receipts for a number of years, which are used to pay bonuses, dividends – and which, most importantly, form a very significant part of bank core capital.

It is clear that leverage must build up in such a system where capital consists of unearned future payments, and costs and dividends must be funded out of additional

borrowings as a result. Given this, it is amazing that more focus has not been placed on this area by regulators trying to stabilise the banking system.

The key flaw in current accounting rules is the following: while it provides welcome transparency and useful information to show financial instruments at face value on the balance sheet, it is a fallacy to suggest that any change in the balance sheet carrying value of an asset or liability should be recognised as profit and loss. In the days when the principle of prudence was a core accounting assumption, a distinction was made between earned income (profits) and revaluation reserves.

The tools still exist for this today – the difference between comprehensive income and profit is essentially an unrealised revaluation reserve.

In my opinion, one of the most crucial reforms that could be made

to restore stability to the banking system is to restore this distinction between earned income and unearned mark-to-market valuation changed. Financial assets and liabilities should be shown at fair value on the balance sheet, with the changes in fair value recognised initially in comprehensive income.

However, such changes in valuation should not be recognised as profit in the income statement – and therefore become distributable to shareholders as dividends or employees as bonuses – until they become properly earned and converted into cash or on an accruals basis over the life of the instrument.

This amortisation of income over the life of the instrument should apply to all types arrangements that currently allow profits to be booked up front on a long-term instrument: witness, for example, the practice of charging a high up-front "arrangement fee" (coupled with a

relatively reduced rate of interest) for a long-term loan – where the reality is that the arrangement fee represents part of the interest cost of the loan over its life, but is structured that way to maximise the immediate accounting profits recognised from making a loan.

Accounting rules must reflect the simple economic fact that banks make profits when they receive their money back, not when they lend it out. The current accounting fiction that regards short-term mark-to-market changes in value as realised profit, regardless of what risks there may be to receiving the cash in the future, is extremely dangerous.

This system was and remains a fundamental factor contributing to the instability of the financial system and is in urgent need of reform.

Paul Phillips,
Partner,
Londinium Capital Partners,
London EC3, UK

★

Congrat

The Motorola CLIQ has stopped me dead in my tracks, and happ so. It's a great device with some unique features in a hardware design that is very functional.... In the end, the strong social networking and messaging features make the CLIQ an absolute winner, and one that will likely earn a permanent position in my own pocket. I give it a "Highly Recommended" rating.

—MobileBurn

is a fraction of the purchase price of the new Capex. So the decline in new equipment depreciation expense in the Income Statement (and therefore its impact on EPS) will take more time to become apparent because (a) the company is transferring only a fraction of the actual Capex cost and (b) the remaining plant and equipment will continue to be depreciated each period. The combined effect of (a) and (b) will mute the impact of Capex Transfer on EPS. On the other hand, Free Cash Flow per share will benefit quickly from the actual decline in Capex. FCS, therefore, will show the impact of Capex Transfer faster than EPS. Outsourcing to overseas subcontractors is just one example of Capex Transfer.

IHOP, the pancake restaurant, dramatically increased FCS by moving from owning its restaurants to a franchise model. When it owned the restaurants, IHOP had to fund both new restaurant construction and existing restaurants' maintenance Capex. Once IHOP transferred the Capex burden to franchise owners, it could focus on value-added uses of capital, such as menu design and quality control. Capex Transfer is not going to turn a pig into a princess but it can often help investor return.

CAPEX AND INVESTOR RETURN

Capex is an important determinant of investor return. According to the description of the Schwab Equity Rating model in the *Barron's* article mentioned earlier, the higher a company's Capex spending, the lower the returns on the company's stock.[3] Many investors do not appreciate how difficult it is to conceive, plan, and execute a major Capex project. Meeting project budgets and completion targets is often challenging, especially if the management team is executing a particular type of project for the first time. If it is the fifth time they are building a new plant or buying a complex automated equipment cell, they may well complete the project without any major surprises. But if it is the first time, watch out. Sometimes the magnitude of a project disaster is so large it materially affects the company's overall results. A chronically high Capex level means there is little room for management mistakes or bad luck. But even companies that do an excellent job of managing Capex year in and year out will find it difficult to generate acceptable investor returns if Capex levels are too high.

FREE CASH FLOW

Chapter 3 laid out the benefits of using Free Cash Flow and pointed out some users of Free Cash Flow. In this chapter we looked at the components of Free Cash Flow. This chapter has argued it is a mistake to focus only on the Free Cash Flow *number itself*. To fully exploit the advantages of Free Cash Flow over EPS, the investor must use the Free Cash Flow Statement. The Free Cash Flow Statement more quickly reflects major changes in company operations, such as Capex Transfer, that affect investor returns. What is more critical to investor success than perceiving important changes in a company's prospects *before* other investors see them? Also, the Free Cash Flow Statement is somewhat less vulnerable, although *definitely not immune*, to accounting fraud and exploitation of GAAP's gaps. On the other hand, the Free Cash Flow investor must pay more attention than the EPS investor to management manipulation of Working Capital.

FREE CASH FLOW YIELD

Many investors use the Price Earning (PE) Ratio to calculate stock price targets. They first estimate next year's EPS and then multiply the EPS estimate by the stock's PE Ratio. We will use the Free Cash Flow Yield to estimate the impact on share price of changes in share value resulting from projected changes in Free Cash Flow per share.

$$\text{Free Cash Flow Yield} = \frac{\text{Free Cash Flow per share}}{\text{Stock Price}} \qquad (4.5)$$

In Chapter 5, we cover the key changes in a company's financial structure that affect share value. We assume interest rates do not change during our projection period. And of course, like all equity valuation schemes, we assume share value is recognized sooner or later by the market in a company's share price.

Let's say ABC Corporation's stock price is $38. We know ABC's Free Cash Flow per share is $2.42. Therefore ABC's Free Cash Flow Yield is:

$$\text{Free Cash Flow Yield} = \frac{\text{Free Cash Flow per share}}{\text{Stock Price}}$$

$$= \frac{\$2.42}{\$38} = 6\% \qquad (4.6)$$

We use Free Cash Flow Yield to estimate the change in stock price resulting from our estimate of future changes in a company's operations: the difference between current Free Cash Flow per share and our estimate of next year's Free Cash Flow per share. Let's say our estimate of ABC's Free Cash Flow per share (FCS) next year is $2.70 (our worksheet will help us project Free Cash Flow when we work with McDonald's in Chapter 6). Here is the formula to estimate the impact of a change in Free Cash Flow per share on the company's share value:

$$\Delta \text{ Share Value due to Operations}$$

$$= \frac{(\text{Next Year's FCS} - \text{Current Year's FCS})}{\text{Current Year's FCS}}$$

$$= \frac{(\$2.70 - \$2.42)}{\$2.42} = 12\% \tag{4.7}$$

Since ABC's stock price is $38, a 12 percent increase in share value amounts to $4.56. However, our 12 percent return estimate is only one of the three drivers that will influence ABC's future stock price. The 12 percent estimate only reflects the change in ABC's stock price resulting from the change in Free Cash Flow generated by company *operations*. The 12 percent estimate does *not* include (a) changes in the company's *financial structure* and (b) changes in *interest rates*. Since we are dealing with (a) in Chapter 5, let's briefly look at interest rates and their role in equity prices.

Note that the Free Cash Flow Yield is an inverse, cash flow version of the Price Earnings Ratio (PE).

$$\text{Price-Earnings Ratio (PE)} = \frac{\text{Stock Price}}{\text{Earnings per share}} \tag{4.8}$$

If we invert the PE Ratio, we get the Earnings Ratio:

$$\text{Earnings Ratio} = \frac{\text{Earnings per share}}{\text{Stock Price}} \tag{4.9}$$

The Earnings Ratio and the Free Cash Flow Yield are the same ratio except that the former uses EPS and the latter uses Free Cash Flow per share (FCS).

In the book *Free Cash Flow and Shareholder Yield: New Priorities for the Global Investor,* Bill Priest and Lindsay McClelland point out that "... inflation expectations drive long-term interest rates, and long-term interest rates are the discounting mechanism for future cash flows/earnings and are the driver of P/E ratios."[4]

We assume that interest rates drive Free Cash Flow Yields in approximately the same manner they drive Earnings Ratios. We also assume a constant Free Cash Flow Yield and in doing so assume constant interest rates. But if we buy a stock based on our company estimates and our use of the Free Cash Flow Yield, the stock price could still drop significantly even though the company met both our operations and financial estimates and there were no material negative news about the company. That's because if interest rates increase materially while we own the stock, the Free Cash Flow Yield will increase, everything else being equal. Here's ABC's new Free Cash Flow Yield at the higher $2.70 Free Cash Flow per share number after interest rates increased and equity prices declined:

$$\text{Free Cash Flow Yield} = \frac{\text{Free Cash Flow per share}}{\text{Stock Price}}$$

$$= \frac{\$2.70}{\$33} = 8\% \qquad (4.10)$$

There are several advantages in using a stock's Free Cash Flow Yield rather than its price multiple. First, yields and interest rates act together. When interest rates go up, yields go up and vice versa. And when yields go up, stock prices go down. Stocks are not as different from bonds as some investors think. Market PEs, however, generally increase when interest rates decline and decrease when interest rates climb. In Chapter 1, we touched on a second advantage yields have over multiples. The Return Multiple uses yield comparisons to help us get a handle on relative return and risk.

The Free Cash Flow Statement provides the investor with a much clearer picture than does the Income Statement of how effectively management is employing investor capital in a company's operations. Still, the investor needs to know more. The investor needs to understand how a company's deployment of its Free Cash Flow is likely to affect share value and potential investor return. Chapter 5 covers deployments. In Chapter 6 we use the Free Cash Flow Worksheet and apply what we have learned about Free Cash Flow and deployments to McDonald's.

CHAPTER 5

Free Cash Flow Deployment

Estimating a company's future Free Cash Flow is the first step in maximizing investor return. The second step is to understand the extent to which the company's deployment of Free Cash Flow is likely to increase or reduce share value and thereby increase or reduce investor return. We do not want to invest in companies that generate a lot of Free Cash Flow but then deploy the Free Cash Flow in ways that trash share value.

Management can deploy a company's Free Cash Flow among four major alternatives:

- Acquisitions
- Stock buybacks
- Dividends
- Debt reduction

Some investors include *new* Capex (Capex for new capacity) as the fifth deployment, limiting the Capex component of Free Cash Flow to *maintenance* Capex. We do not categorize new Capex as a deployment for two reasons. It is difficult to obtain a breakdown of new Capex and maintenance Capex in public company disclosures. Most companies do not provide Capex breakdowns in their disclosures and guidance. We have seen suggestions as to how to estimate the breakdown but we are not comfortable with such estimates. Second, even if a company did provide a breakdown, we conservatively assume our Revenues projection depends on total projected Capex. To do otherwise is to overstate Free Cash Flow. The direct connection between Revenues and total Capex is not shared by the four aforementioned deployments. Having said that, the utility of Free Cash Flow can only be increased by its continuous improvement and refinement. Those investors who prefer to include new Capex in deployments rather than in the Free Cash Flow Statement should modify the worksheet. It is hoped that those investors who increase returns by modifying the worksheet will share their success with other readers at www.OakdaleAdvisors.com.

Before we focus on the four deployments, we will consider deployment of Free Cash Flow in a broader conceptual context. First, positive Free Cash Flow is not a prerequisite for any of the four deployments. A company with negative Free Cash Flow can fund any or all of the four deployments by issuing new debt or new equity or both. Second, a company with positive Free Cash Flow can fund total deployments that exceed its Free Cash Flow by issuing new debt or new equity or both. Third, a company need not deploy its Free Cash Flow. Free Cash Flow can accumulate in the cash and marketable securities accounts. Fourth, a company can return all of its Free Cash Flow to its operations rather than deploy it to any of the four alternatives. Many good companies generate the entire investor return from increases in Free Cash Flow per share.

To keep things simple, we will again use ABC Corporation as an example. We refer to the Free Cash Flow Worksheet in this chapter without showing it. We do that to lay the groundwork for the introduction of the worksheet in the next chapter.

ACQUISITIONS

The mechanics of dealing with acquisitions are straightforward. For starters, we hope the acquired company generates Free Cash Flow! We divide the acquired company's estimated Free Cash Flow by the acquirer's number of shares after the acquisition. Let's say ABC is going to buy the XYZ Company. XYZ's expected annual Free Cash Flow is $4 million.

ABC is not using its stock to pay for XYZ so we will use ABC's 20 million shares.

Acquired Company's Contribution to Acquirer's FCS

$$= \frac{\text{Acquired Company's FCF}}{\text{Acquirer's Number of Shares}} = \frac{\$4 \text{ Million}}{20 \text{ Million}} = \$0.20 \text{ FCS} \quad (5.1)$$

The worksheet will add our estimate of the Free Cash Flow per share contributed by the acquired company to our estimate of the buyer's Free Cash Flow per share. Then the worksheet will calculate the impact on share value of the *total* change in the buyer's estimated Free Cash Flow per share (FCS) resulting from the company's existing operations and the acquired company's operations. The equation for the acquired company's effect on share value is the same equation we used for the impact on share value of a change in ABC's Free Cash Flow per share (equation 4.6).

$$\Delta \text{ Share Value due to Acquisition}$$

$$= \frac{\text{Acquired Company's FCS}}{\text{Acquirer's FCS}} = \frac{\$0.20}{\$2.42} = 8\% \qquad (5.2)$$

Now we add the acquired company's estimated Free Cash Flow per share to the existing operations.

$$\Delta \text{ Share Value due to Operations and Acquisition}$$

$$= \frac{\Delta \text{ in Operation's FCS} + \text{Acquired Company's FCS}}{\text{Acquirer's FCS}}$$

$$= \frac{(\$0.28 + \$0.20)}{\$2.42} = \frac{\$0.48}{\$2.42} = 20\% \qquad (5.3)$$

The acquired company alone is estimated to add $0.20 incremental Free Cash Flow per share. The $0.20 increase would increase share value by 8 percent ($0.20 divided by $2.42). The two companies combined are expected to generate $0.48 in additional Free Cash Flow per share for a 20 percent increase in share value. The 20 percent increase addresses *only* the combined companies' incremental Free Cash Flow per share. The 20 percent will initially decline to the extent the acquisition is financed by debt or new equity.

We will input the amount of cash used to make the acquisition in our worksheet. If common shares are used to pay for the acquisition, those added shares will be included in our estimate of the change in the number of shares. We will cover that in the next section of this chapter. If debt is used to pay for the acquisition, the additional debt will be included in our estimate of the change in total debt. We also discuss debt later in this chapter.

Where do we get the acquired company's Free Cash Flow estimate? If there are sell-side analyst reports on the company, we can see their estimates of the seller's Free Cash Flow. We also need to look at the seller's financials and compute a Free Cash Flow estimate. The worksheet will help us compute a Free Cash Flow estimate.

Unfortunately, acquisitions often reduce rather than increase share value and investor returns. Some acquisitions made within the same industry and with either geographical or product line overlap have a chance at succeeding because there are material opportunities for a reduction of overhead and for cost savings because of the now-larger scale. But acquisitions made outside the buyer's core business often indicate management thinks its core business offers less than acceptable prospects. If that is the case, management goes on an acquisition hunt to find another type of business with more attractive prospects. That frequently means the acquired company must perform after the acquisition at a level that overcompensates for the anemic results of the buyer's core business and pays for the premium price often paid by the buyer. The management of the buyer is not really knowledgeable about the business of the seller. That means the buyer overestimates synergies and underestimates the difficulties in combining the two companies. Investors should not assume any synergies unless they know the industry and are convinced there will be real synergies. Frequently, realized synergies, if any, are offset by unexpected problems in the integration of the two companies. Time spent in the acquisition process is time not spent on the core business. Having said all that, some companies have an excellent acquisition track record. The best prospects are those companies that do relatively small deals and have successfully done a lot of them in their core business.

When reading about an M&A deal, we will usually see a reference to the proposed deal's *accretive* or *dilutive* impact on EPS. This refers to how much the deal increases or decreases the buyer's EPS. It is irrelevant to Free Cash Flow investors whether the projections say the deal is accretive or dilutive. First, investor return comes from Free Cash Flow and its deployment, not EPS. Second, most acquisitions are accretive anyway since the FASB generously changed the rules for amortizing acquisition goodwill. Goodwill amortization used to be done automatically. Now it is only done when, in hindsight, management decides the assumptions employed in accounting for the acquisition are no longer valid.

BUYBACKS

We estimate the amount of cash a company will deploy into buybacks, if any. The worksheet divides our cash deployment estimate by the stock price and gives us the number of shares removed from the market by the buybacks.

$$\text{Number of Shares Purchased} = \frac{\text{Amount Deployed for Buybacks}}{\text{Stock Price}} \quad (5.4)$$

It would be great if we could stop here, but we must also estimate the amount of cash received by the issuance of any new shares. New shares are issued for a follow-on stock issue (also known as a secondary issue), the exercise of employee stock options, and to pay for acquisitions, among other things.

$$\text{Number of Shares Issued} = \frac{\text{Amount Received from Shares Issued}}{\text{Stock Price}} \quad (5.5)$$

Our worksheet takes the aforementioned changes and nets them against the most recent number of shares outstanding.

Estimated Number of Shares Outstanding at End of Year

= Prior Period's Number of Shares Outstanding

− Number of Shares Purchased + Number of Shares Issued (5.6)

The worksheet then takes our Free Cash Flow estimate and computes the change in Free Cash Flow per share resulting from the change in the number of shares. Excluding the acquisition of XYZ, we know ABC is expected to have a Free Cash Flow per share of $2.70 next year and that it now has 20 million shares outstanding. Free Cash Flow will be $54 million. We expect the total number of shares outstanding to drop by 200,000 shares over the course of the year and end up at 19.8 million shares.

$$
\begin{aligned}
\text{Estimated } &\Delta \text{ in FCS Due to } \Delta \text{ in Number of Shares} \\
&= \frac{\text{Estimated Free Cash Flow}}{\text{Estimated Number of Shares at Year-End}} \\
&\quad - \frac{\text{Estimated Free Cash Flow}}{\text{Prior Period's Number of Shares}} \\
&= \frac{\$54 \text{ Million}}{19.8 \text{ Million}} - \frac{\$54 \text{ Million}}{20 \text{ Million}} \\
&= \$2.73 - \$2.70 = \$0.03 \text{ per share} \quad (5.7)
\end{aligned}
$$

In other words, if ABC had *not* reduced its total number of shares by 200,000, its Free Cash Flow per share would be $2.70. But it did, so ABC's Free Cash Flow per share is $2.73.

We next estimate the increase in share value resulting from the decrease in the number of shares outstanding. All we do is divide our estimate of the net change in the number of shares by the prior period's number of total shares. We multiply the 200,000 decrease by −1 to convert the decrease into an increase in share value.

$$\Delta \text{ Share Value due to } \Delta \text{ in Number of Shares}$$
$$= \frac{\text{Net } \Delta \text{ in Number of Shares}}{\text{Prior Period's Number of Shares}} = \frac{200,000}{20 \text{ million}} = 1\% \quad (5.8)$$

There are six types of stock buybacks. Unfortunately, only one of the six always enhances share value. The six types of buybacks are:

Nonbuybacks, which are announced by the company in a press release but the company does not buy back a material amount of its stock. The press release is the beginning and the end of the buybacks. Investors must avoid CEOs who do nonbuybacks.

Bonus buybacks, which are implemented by CEOs to increase EPS so that the CEO can meet the EPS target in his bonus or compensation package. While investors may well benefit from the decline in the number of shares, all too often the CEO manages to more than offset the buyback's benefits by wreaking economic havoc elsewhere in the company's operations and finances. GAAP accounting's complexity and lack of transparency afford ample opportunities for a CEO to sacrifice the company's (and investors') economic best interests for personal gain. Some EPS investors are clueless when it comes to bonus buybacks. Many market commentators have complained that a recent buyback surge did not help the companies' stock prices. Of course, buybacks do not benefit investors when a CEO attempts to buy back his bonus while at the same time destroying more share value in his company than whatever share value increase resulted from the bonus buybacks! The stock price will eventually reflect the effects of both the buybacks and the economic pillaging.

Defensive buybacks, which are done by CEOs who want to increase EPS (and often debt) to ward off potential nonfriendly acquirers. We look at defensive buybacks the same way we look at bonus buybacks: They serve the CEO's short-term interests while often destroying share value.

Front door buybacks, which look great to some investors at first glance because these investors are standing in the company's front yard. These investors do not see all the new shares moving out the company's back door. Frequently, the new shares issued for the exercise of employee stock options materially reduce the beneficial impact of buybacks on investor return. Some CEO's brag about the buybacks without mentioning the stock option exercises.

Delusional buybacks, which are done by companies with negative Free Cash Flow. These grotesque buybacks result in investors owning a larger share of a company's negative Free Cash Flow. Some EPS investors say

"Thanks!" to CEOs who do delusional buybacks. Free Cash Flow investors say "Thanks but NO THANKS!"

Investor buybacks, which are the only buybacks that actually increase total investor return. Investor buybacks are not nonbuybacks, bonus buybacks, defensive buybacks, front-door buybacks or delusional buybacks. It should come as no surprise that investor buybacks are funded with Free Cash Flow and/or cash and marketable securities. Debt-financed buybacks are frequently bonus buybacks or defensive buybacks. The Free Cash Flow Worksheet helps the investor determine the return tradeoff between the FCS benefit of a debt-financed buyback and the negative impact of the additional debt. The investor's time horizon will have a large impact on the outcome of a trade-off analysis. If the debt is expected to be fully repaid in one year and the investor intends to hold the stock (subject to annual review) for more than a year, then the debt-financed buyback may make sense. Of course, unexpected events can make it impossible for the company to pay off the debt in the expected time frame. Investor beware.

DIVIDENDS

ABC pays $1.50 annual dividend. Here is the formula for dividend yield.

$$\text{Dividend Yield} = \frac{\text{Dividend}}{\text{Stock Price}} = \frac{\$1.50}{\$38} = 3.9\% \qquad (5.9)$$

Dividends are fantastic. The cash can be spent or the dividend can be reinvested in the company's stock or other investments. Dividend reinvestment can add significantly to investor return. Professor Jeremy Siegel's *The Future for Investors: Why the Tried and the True Triumph over the Bold and the New* lays out a compelling case for dividend reinvestment based on extensive research of the S&P 500 and other data.[1] If only we could end our discussion of dividends right here, but we cannot. Relax, we are not going to list six types of dividends. Thankfully, dividends do not require a list. But *investors* who buy stocks *primarily* because of their dividend yields require a list and here it is.

Five Investor Diseases
1. Dividend Psychosis
2. Dividend Hyperfocus
3. Dividend Fixation
4. Dividendmania
5. Dividenditis

EPS investors are especially vulnerable to dividend disease. That is because unlike most of the moving parts in GAAP financials—the accruals, restatements, and other accounting mysteries—dividends are unusually straightforward and understandable. The Free Cash Flow investor is also very fond of dividends, but the Free Cash Flow investor buys a stock only when the *combined impact* of Free Cash Flow *and* its deployment is likely to lead to acceptable returns. If a company is paying dividends but Free Cash Flow per share appears to be headed south for the foreseeable future or deployment is sabotaging investor return, the Free Cash Flow investor looks elsewhere for companies likely to increase overall investor return.

DEBT

We estimate in our worksheet the impact of the change in a company's total debt outstanding on share value by first adding estimated Free Cash Flow and other sources of cash. Then we subtract our estimates of the company's deployments for acquisitions, buybacks, dividends, and scheduled debt repayments.

$$\Delta \text{ in Debt} = \text{Free Cash Flow} + \text{Other Sources of Cash} - \text{Deployments}$$

$$(5.10)$$

If deployments exceed total sources of cash, we assume the difference is funded by additional debt. If sources of cash exceed deployments, we assume the difference is used to repay existing debt, if any. We go into more detail on this subject in Chapter 6.

Let's assume we have already estimated ABC's total debt is likely to drop by $15 million. We will use the $15 million number to derive the change in share value. The worksheet first divides the $15 million Δ in debt by the total number of shares outstanding to get the Δ in debt per share.

$$\text{Estimated } \Delta \text{ in Debt per share} = \frac{\text{Estimated } \Delta \text{ in Debt}}{\text{Number of Shares}}$$

$$= \frac{(\$15 \text{ million})}{19.8 \text{ million}} = (\$0.76) \text{ per share} \qquad (5.11)$$

We use the Δ in debt decrease of ($0.76) to compute the estimated change in share value. Please note: usually financial numbers in parentheses convey a *negative* meaning—but a decrease in total debt is a *positive* event.

$$\Delta \text{ in Share Value due to } \Delta \text{ in Debt} = \frac{\Delta \text{ Debt per share}}{\text{Stock Price}}$$

$$= \frac{(\$0.76)}{\$38} = 2\% \qquad (5.12)$$

Recall our discussion of the outdoor furniture company and how the use of debt affects investors. The lower the total debt balance, the larger the claim investors have on the company's ongoing Free Cash Flow and on the sale proceeds when the company is sold. For that reason, in their discounted cash flow models, sell-side analysts subtract a company's debt balance from their estimate of the present value of the company's projected Free Cash Flows and terminal value. Basic finance courses teach that debt reduces a company's cost of capital and therefore the discount rate used to discount future cash flows. Debt also has tax benefits because investment interest is tax deductible. As the Free Cash Flow Worksheet does not incorporate many corporate finance concepts, investors who employ cost of capital or other tools can modify the Free Cash Flow Worksheet to accommodate their preferred metrics.

Let's repeat what we said about the use of debt to fund buybacks but this time apply it to the use of debt generally: The investor's time horizon will have a large impact on the outcome of a debt analysis. If the new debt is expected to be fully repaid in, say, one year and the investor intends to hold the stock (subject to annual review) for more than a year, then the new debt may make eminent sense. Of course, unexpected events can make it impossible for the company to pay off the debt in the expected time frame. Everything else being equal, the risks, restrictions and costs of debt suggest that companies that can grow Free Cash Flow without the need of additional debt may be better investments than those companies that require debt to grow.

We are not anti-debt. Sometimes the best possible course of action is to increase debt. All we are trying to do is quantify the potential impact of changes in total debt on investor return and investor risk. Having done that, we can then consider how much incremental return we are receiving for the amount of incremental risk we are taking. Not having done that, where are we?

PROJECTING INVESTOR RETURN

The Free Cash Flow investor looks at a company's total return potential. We laid out in the last chapter and in this chapter each of the components of ABC's total return potential. We now bring together all of the equations that reflect a change in share value to obtain a total investor return estimate for ABC Corporation.

Step 1: Δ Share Value due to Operations

In Chapter 4 we estimated how an increase or decrease in the Free Cash Flow generated by ABC's existing operations will affect share value.

$$\Delta \text{ Share Value due to Operations}$$
$$= \frac{(\text{Next Year's FCS} - \text{Current Year's FCS})}{\text{Current Year's FCS}}$$
$$= \frac{(\$2.70 - \$2.42)}{\$2.42} = 12\% \qquad (4.6)$$

Step 2: Δ Share Value due to Acquisition

If the company is doing an acquisition, we estimate how the acquired company's Free Cash Flow will affect ABC's share value.

$$\Delta \text{ Share Value due to Acquisition}$$
$$= \frac{\text{Acquired Company's FCS}}{\text{Acquirer's FCS}} = \frac{\$0.20}{\$2.42} = 8\% \qquad (5.2)$$

Step 3: Δ Share Value due to Δ in the Number of Shares

Next is the impact on share value of the change in the total number of shares outstanding. We want to keep the change in total shares separate from the change in Free Cash Flow per share from operations and acquisitions. This separation provides a clearer window on two entirely different sources of return: the operational generation of incremental Free Cash Flow versus the share change number. To keep things simple, we assume the acquisition was funded entirely by cash and marketable securities.

$$\Delta \text{ Share Value due to } \Delta \text{ in Number of Shares}$$
$$= \frac{\text{Net } \Delta \text{ in Number of Shares}}{\text{Prior Period's Number of Shares}} = \frac{200,000}{20 \text{ million}} = 1\% \qquad (5.8)$$

EXHIBIT 5.1 ABC Corporation's Investor Return Projection

	Investor Return
Δ Share Value due to Operations	12%
Δ Share Value due to Acquisitions	8%
Δ Share Value due to Δ in Number of shares	1%
Dividend Yield	4%
Δ Share Value due to Δ in Total debt	2%
Total Investor Return	27%

Step 4: Dividend Yield

Here's the easiest part.

$$\text{Dividend Yield} = \frac{\text{Dividend}}{\text{Stock Price}} = \frac{\$1.50}{\$38} = 4\% \qquad (5.9)$$

Step 5: Δ Share Value due to Δ in Debt

Here's the last part.

$$\Delta \text{ in Share Value due to } \Delta \text{ in Debt} = \frac{\Delta \text{ Debt per share}}{\text{Stock Price}}$$

$$= \frac{(\$0.76)}{\$38} = 2\% \qquad (5.12)$$

We now bring together the five sources of investor return to obtain our estimate of total investor return (see Exhibit 5.1).

Without the acquisition, the total return estimate would be 19 percent. The relative size of each of the five components is important. In this regard, the investor must look at each company individually and make a judgment based on the company's prospects. Just for fun, let's see what happens if we turn the returns in Exhibit 5.1 upside down. What do we think about the resulting changes in component returns?

The total investor return estimate in Exhibit 5.2 is the same as Exhibit 5.1 but the components' percentages are much less appealing. The 2 percent Operations return leaves a lot to be desired. There are countless companies that have stronger prospects. The 8 percent dividend yield might thrill those afflicted by *dividenditis*. Also, is it not less than inspiring that the 12 percent

EXHIBIT 5.2   ABC Corporation's Investor Return Projection (Version 2)

	Investor Return
Δ Share Value due to Operations	2%
Δ Share Value due to Acquisitions	4%
Δ Share Value due to Δ in Number of shares	1%
Dividend Yield	8%
Δ Share Value due to Δ in Total debt	12%
Total Investor Return	27%

debt reduction return is the largest source of return? It is necessary to look at a large number of investor return estimates to develop a feel for various component mixes in different industries.

In the next chapter, we apply what we have learned about Free Cash Flow and deployment to McDonald's. After entering McDonald's historical financials into the worksheet, we will do a one-year projection of McDonald's Free Cash Flow and deployments.

CHAPTER 6

The Free Cash Flow Worksheet

We said in the Introduction that the Free Cash Flow Worksheet was created for this book. Because it is new, the Free Cash Flow Worksheet should be viewed as a "work in progress." The author welcomes all suggestions and criticisms for the improvement of the worksheet. Please visit the author's web site (www.OakdaleAdvisors.com) to share your insights and see other readers' comments.

Using the Free Cash Flow Worksheet is certainly not the only way to understand and use Free Cash Flow and deployment. But there is a big difference between just reading this book and also trying out the worksheet. Using the worksheet tests your comprehension of Free Cash Flow and deployment. It can also give you a better appreciation of the strengths and limitations of the worksheet design and the formulas. The Free Cash Flow Worksheet should be used as an add-on or overlay to the investor's existing analytics. It is not intended to be the investor's sole quantitative analysis of a company. The formulas in the worksheet do not handle all possible situations. Be especially careful when working with companies that have unusually large changes from one year to the next. *Because the Free Cash Flow Worksheet is new, your investor return projections should be used only as one part of a comprehensive equity analysis that also includes conventional analytics such as EPS/PE or the DCF model.*

This chapter explains what data we need to use the worksheet, where we obtain the data, where in the worksheet we input the data, and what the worksheet does with the data. There are two downloadable Excel files available at www.wiley.com/go/christy. The Six Restaurants file has been completed using the financial data of McDonald's and five other restaurant companies. The Free Cash Flow Worksheet file has the same format and formulas as the Six Restaurants file, but has no company data. Use the Free Cash Flow Worksheet file to work on your own companies.

We will see how McDonald's generated and deployed its Free Cash Flow in the years 2004–2006. Then we will use the worksheet's formulas to estimate McDonald's 2007 Free Cash Flow, deployments, and investor return. Our McDonald's' estimates and our estimates for the other companies were done in mid-2007 only to demonstrate how to use the worksheet. We used some 2007 company data in making the estimates. Such data would not have been available in late 2006–early 2007 to an analyst estimating 2007 results. In any event, your use of the worksheet, your judgments, your due diligence, your analysis, and therefore your results will certainly differ from ours.

Finally, while we explain each Row in the worksheet, we will not necessarily explain each Row in sequential order. We will skip some Rows but eventually return to explain them.

WORKSHEET FEATURES

Before we explain the worksheet Row by Row, let's first take a look at the Cash Sources section of the McDonald's worksheet (see Exhibit 6.1) so we can point out some of the worksheet's features.

Column A holds the Row titles. Some of the Row titles in Rows 82–92 are in a regular type font and some are in a **bold font.** Regular font Row titles are built into the spreadsheet. The Row titles in **bold font** are specific to the company being modeled, in this case McDonald's, and were typed into the blank cells. When you are working on your own company in the Free Cash Flow Worksheet, you will use some of the blank Column A title cells to type in Row titles specific to your company.

	A	C	D	E
82	CASH SOURCES AND CASH DEPLOYMENTS			
83	CASH SOURCES	2006	2005	2004
84	Free Cash Flow	$ 2,662.6	$ 2,814.2	$ 2,582.3
85	**Sale of assets**	597.4	259.1	306.3
86	**Borrowings**	36.4	3,130.6	261.5
87	**Stock options exercised**	975.7	768.1	580.5
88				
89				
90				
91				
92	Total Cash Sources	$ 4,272.1	$ 6,972.0	$ 3,730.6
93				

EXHIBIT 6.1 Worksheet Features

Column B, the projection year Column, has been temporarily hidden so it is not a distraction while we do McDonald's 2004–2006 historical financials. When we are finished with the historical numbers, we will open Column B to work on the 2007 projection. When you work on your own companies in the worksheet, Column B will not be hidden. As you are entering historical numbers in Columns C–E, strange numbers will appear in some Column B cells. Ignore them. When you work on the projection and enter numbers in Column B, the strange numbers will disappear as the worksheet's formulas go to work on your inputs.

Why in Exhibit 6.1 do the years in Row 83 run chronologically backward, left to right, from 2006 to 2004? Because the Columns in most public companies' financial statements run backward. Our worksheets follow this accounting convention so your transfer of data from your companies' financial statements to the worksheet is as easy as possible. The year Column headings have to be entered only once—at the top of the worksheet. The worksheet copies your inputs and enters all of the other year Column headings.

In the completed McDonald's worksheet, the numbers in **bold font** are in cells in which you will enter data in the Free Cash Flow Worksheet when working on your own companies. The numbers *not* in bold are calculated by the worksheet's built-in formulas. In Exhibit 6.2 you will find the same Cash Sources section *before* any company numbers have been entered.

In Exhibit 6.2, cell C85 is highlighted. Enter data *only* in the cells that have either a "0" in them or nothing in Excel's "*fx*" bar above the Column A and B headings (the Exhibits do not show the Excel *fx* bar but you will see them in the worksheet on your computer screen). Cell C85's *fx* bar is blank so data can be put in this cell and the Row title typed in the blank A85 cell.

	A	C	D	E
82	CASH SOURCES AND CASH DEPLOYMENTS			
83	CASH SOURCES	200y	200x	200w
84	Free Cash Flow	$ -	$ -	$ -
85				
86				
87				
88				
89				
90				
91				
92	Total Cash Sources	$ -	$ -	$ -

EXHIBIT 6.2 Cell C85 in Free Cash Flow Worksheet

A	C	D	E
112			
113 Dividends	200y	200x	200w
114 Dividends	$ -	$ -	$ -
115 Weighted avg. shares – diluted	-	-	-
116 Dividend paid per share	#DIV/0!	#DIV/0!	#DIV/0!

EXHIBIT 6.3   Cell C114 in Free Cash Flow Worksheet

Certain cells in the Free Cash Flow Worksheet have a "$" and/or a "—". Be careful: some of these cells have formulas and some do not. Cell C114 in Exhibit 6.3 has a "0" in the *fx* bar so you will enter the amount of dividends paid in C114 if the company paid dividends in whatever year "200y" turns out to be. If Cell C115 were highlighted, "=C39" would appear in the *fx* bar, so do not put data in the cell because the worksheet takes care of this cell. All cells with a "#DIV/O!" or a "N/A" have built-in formulas. If you enter numbers into a cell with a "#DIV/O!" or an "N/A" you will erase the formula in the cell.

ENTERING HISTORICAL DATA

We start at the top of the Six Restaurants file.

> **Row 1:** Exhibit 6.4 is a picture of the first 17 rows. Enter the company's name in Cell A1. You will see that Columns B–E in the Free Cash Flow Worksheet are formatted for companies (like McDonald's) that report their results using numbers with one decimal point, while Columns H–K are formatted for companies that report results in whole numbers.

> **Row 2:** Companies report their results in millions, thousands, or actual numbers. In A2, delete whatever does not apply to the company you are working on. Enter the years or quarters of the historical statements. The worksheet takes your entries and fills in all of the other period column headings.

ADJUSTMENTS TO GAAP CASH FLOW

> **Row 4:** Obtain the company's "Cash provided by operating activities" numbers (Net CFO) from the GAAP Cash Flow. Exhibit 6.5 is McDonald's 2006 GAAP Cash Flow Statement. McDonald's 2006

	A	C	D	E
		2006	**2005**	**2004**
1	**McDonald's**			
2	(000,000's)	**2006**	**2005**	**2004**
3	ADJUSTMENTS TO GAAP CASH FLOW			
4	Cash provided by operating activities (Net CFO)	$ 4,341.5	$ 4,337.0	$ 3,903.6
5				
6	Changes in Working Capital/Other			
7	Accounts receivable	$ (90.8)	$ (56.5)	$ (35.9)
8	Inventories	(1.6)	(29.4)	(14.9)
9	Accounts payable	82.8	35.8	86.7
10	Income taxes	(350.3)	442.9	84.2
11	Other accrued liabilities	196.7	19.5	70.2
12				
13				
14				
15	Total Changes in Working Capital/Other	163.2	(412.3)	(190.3)
16				
17	Operating Cash Flow (OCF)	$ 4,504.7	$ 3,924.7	$ 3,713.3

EXHIBIT 6.4 Entering Historical Data

Income Statement and Balance Sheet are Exhibits B and C in the back of the book. McDonald's calls Net CFO "Cash provided by operations" but it is the same thing as "Cash provided by operating activities."

Row 6: The next step, as shown in Exhibit 6.5, is to remove the Working Capital/Other accounts from the Operating Activities section of the GAAP Cash Flow Statement so that our Net CFO number is devoid of balance sheet change items. The Working Capital changes and other balance sheet accounts are usually indented together at the bottom of the CFO section. McDonald's titles them "Changes in Working Capital items." Some companies use "Changes in operating assets and liabilities" or something similar. In McDonald's case, all of the balance sheet changes are for short-term Working Capital accounts. Many companies also include noncurrent balance sheet changes. Some companies do not include sufficient detail on balance sheet changes in the GAAP Statement, choosing to provide the information in the Notes. We enter *all balance sheet changes* as they appear in the GAAP Cash Flow CFO section (or in the Notes) into the worksheet's Working Capital/Other group in Rows 7–14. If there are not enough blank title rows, add up some of the smaller items in the last blank row using Excel's addition function.

CONSOLIDATED STATEMENT OF CASH FLOWS

IN MILLIONS Years ended December 31,	2006	2005	2004
Operating activities			
Net income	$ 3,544.2	$ 2,602.2	$ 2,278.5
Adjustments to reconcile to cash provided by operations			
Charges and credits			
Depreciation and amortization	1,249.9	1,249.5	1,201.0
Deferred income taxes	28.7	(34.6)	(177.0)
Income taxes audit benefit		(178.8)	
Impairment and other charges (credits), net	134.2	(28.4)	281.4
Gains on Chipotle disposition, net of tax	(653.0)		
Share-based compensation	122.5	152.0	11.0
Other	78.2	162.8	118.4
Changes in working capital items:			
Accounts receivable	(90.8)	(56.5)	(35.9)
Inventories, prepaid expenses and other current assets	(1.6)	(29.4)	(14.9)
Accounts payable	82.8	35.8	86.7
Income taxes	(350.3)	442.9	84.2
Other accrued liabilities	196.7	19.5	70.2
Cash provided by operations	4,341.5	4,337.0	3,903.6
Investing activities			
Property and equipment expenditures	(1,741.9)	(1,606.8)	(1,419.3)
Purchases of restaurant businesses	(238.6)	(343.5)	(149.7)
Sales of restaurant businesses and property	315.7	259.1	306.3
Chipotle disposition	281.7		
Other	109.7	(126.6)	(120.4)
Cash used for investing activities	(1,273.4)	(1,817.8)	(1,383.1)
Financing activities			
Net short-term borrowings (repayments)	34.5	22.7	35.9
Long-term financing issuances	1.9	3,107.9	225.6
Long-term financing repayments	(2,301.1)	(1,518.3)	(1,077.0)
Treasury stock purchases	(2,959.4)	(1,202.0)	(621.0)
Common stock dividends	(1,216.5)	(842.0)	(695.0)
Proceeds from stock option exercises	975.7	768.1	580.5
Excess tax benefit on share-based compensation	87.1	70.1	
Other	185.5	(44.9)	(82.5)
Cash provided by (used for) financing activities	(5,192.3)	361.6	(1,633.5)
Cash and equivalents increase/(decrease)	(2,124.2)	2,880.8	887.0
Cash and equivalents at beginning of year	4,260.6	1,379.8	492.8
Cash and equivalents at end of year	$ 2,136.4	$ 4,260.6	$ 1,379.8
Supplemental cash flow disclosures			
Interest paid	$ 430.3	$ 390.3	$ 370.2
Income taxes paid	1,528.5	795.1	1,017.6

See Notes to consolidated financial statements.

EXHIBIT 6.5 McDonald's Consolidated Statement of Cash Flows

Note: Except for EPS and Net income numbers in Rows 46 and 47, the *Changes in Working Capital / Other* section is the only part of the worksheet in which *negative* numbers in the GAAP Cash Flow Statement are entered as *negative* numbers in the worksheet. In *all* of the other worksheet sections, all *positive and negative* numbers in the GAAP Cash Flow Statement are entered into the worksheet as *positive* numbers.

Investors who are strong in accounting should consider adjusting the Working Capital/Other group so that the following items are excluded:

(1) nonsustainable sources of cash; (2) nonrepetitive uses of cash and (3) nonoperating sources and uses of cash. Consult the book *Creative Cash Flow Reporting* for extensive information on public companies' classifications of sources and uses of cash in the GAAP Cash Flow Statement.[1]

Row 15: The worksheet adds all of the items entered in Rows 7–14 and then multiplies the sum by –1. Why? To get to Operating Cash Flow, we need to back out the Working Capital and other balance sheet accounts from "Cash provided by operating activities." Take McDonald's Accounts receivable as an example. The GAAP Cash Flow has a ($90.8) million change in McDonald's Accounts receivable from 12/31/05 to 12/31/06 because McDonald's Accounts receivable increased $90.8 million from 12/31/05 to 12/31/06. An increase in an asset account is a *use* of cash that is not reflected in the Net Income number, so the GAAP Cash Flow *subtracts* the $90.8 million from Net Income to get to McDonald's "Cash provided by operating activities" (Net CFO) number. Because we want to back out or remove the changes in McDonald's' Working Capital accounts from the Net CFO number, the worksheet multiplies the net change by –1 and adds it to the Net CFO number in Row 4. We will take another look at the –1 when we get to the Free Cash Flow Statement.

OPERATING CASH FLOW

Row 17: The worksheet adds the Net CFO in Row 4 and the Total Changes in Working Capital/Other in Row 15. After the Working Capital/Other changes are removed from the GAAP Cash Flow Statement, all that remains are the charges and credits, such as Depreciation, that are added to or subtracted from Net Income to get to Net CFO. The net of the charges and credit items is the difference between Net Income and our Operating Cash Flow number.

CAPEX

Row 19: In Exhibit 6.6, we entered McDonald's Capex numbers from the Investing section of the GAAP Cash Flow.

Row 21: Enter any adjustments to Capex. McDonald's provided the Capex numbers for Chipotle, a restaurant chain spun off in 2006. We want to remove Chipotle's Capex from McDonald's historical Capex because Chipotle is no longer a part of McDonald's. The

	A	C	D	E
19	Capital expenditures (Capex)	$ 1,741.9	$ 1,606.8	$ 1,419.3
20	Adjustments to Capex :			.
21	**Remove Chipotle Capex**	63.0	84.0	98.0
22	Adjusted Capex	$ 1,678.9	$ 1,522.8	$ 1,321.3

EXHIBIT 6.6   Capex

Cheesecake Factory obtains landlord contributions for its leasehold improvements so we reduce Cheesecake's Capex number by those amounts. If a company is doing capital equipment leases, as is IHOP, we add the new capital leases here because new assets financed by capital leases are not included in the Capex line in GAAP's Cash Flow Statement.

Row 22: The worksheet calculates the effect of the Row 21 adjustment(s), if any, to get Adjusted Capex. If you are adding the number in Row 20, change the minus sign in Row 22's formula to a plus sign ("+").

FROM THE BALANCE SHEET

Rows 25–27+30: Get these numbers from the balance sheet. This group of Rows in Exhibit 6.7 contains the *balances* of these balance sheet accounts as of the date of the balance sheet. These are not *change* numbers. The worksheet will use the three Working Capital numbers to project 2007 Δ Working Capital as a percentage of Revenues. The worksheet will use the debt balance to project both the 2007 interest cost and the change in debt balance in 2007.

	A	C	D	E
22	Adjusted Capex	$ 1,678.9	$ 1,522.8	$ 1,321.3
23				
24	FROM THE BALANCE SHEET			
25	Accounts receivable	$ 904.2	$ 793.9	$ 745.5
26	Inventories	149.0	144.3	147.5
27	Accounts payable	834.1	678.0	714.3
28	Net of receivables, inventories and payables	219.1	260.2	178.7
29	Net as % of Revenues	1%	1%	1%
30	Total debt	$ 8,434.2	$ 9,592.8	

EXHIBIT 6.7   From the Balance Sheet

	A	C	D	E
31				
32	FREE CASH FLOW STATEMENT	2006	2005	2004
33	Revenues	$ 21,586.4	$ 19,832.5	$ 18,594.0
34	Cash Operating Costs	17,081.7	15,907.8	14,880.7
35	Operating Cash Flow (OCF)	4,504.7	3,924.7	3,713.3
36	Δ Working Capital	163.2	(412.3)	(190.3)
37	Capex	1,678.9	1,522.8	1,321.3
38	Free Cash Flow (FCF)	$ 2,662.6	$ 2,814.2	$ 2,582.3
39				
40	Weighted avg. shares - diluted	1,251.7	1,274.2	1,273.7
41	Free Cash Flow per share (FCS)	$ 2.13	$ 2.21	$ 2.03

EXHIBIT 6.8 The Free Cash Flow Statement

THE FREE CASH FLOW STATEMENT

Row 33: Exhibit 6.8 contains the Free Cash Flow Statement. All we need to do is enter the historical Revenues numbers. The worksheet computes all of the other historical rows in the Free Cash Flow Statement.

Row 34: The worksheet calculates Cash Operating Costs (Revenues minus Operating Cash Flow).

Rows 35–37: The worksheet brings down Operating Cash Flow, Δ Working Capital and Capex from Rows 17, 15, and 22, respectively. Note: if Δ Working Capital in Row 36 is a positive number, that means Working Capital increased from the last period. An increase in Working Capital uses cash, so the worksheet *subtracts* a positive number in Row 36 from Operating Cash Flow. A negative Δ Working Capital number (a source of cash) is *added* to Operating Cash Flow. Recall the Accounts receivable example above. We will now assume for purposes of explanation that Accounts receivable is the *only account* in McDonald's Working Capital. Accounts receivable increased from 2005 to 2006. That increase consumed $90.8 million in cash, so there is a ($90.8) million number in the GAAP Cash Flow and in C7 of the worksheet. The formula in Row 15 multiplies the ($90.8) million number by −1 so it becomes a positive number: $90.8 million. If we were to look at the Free Cash Flow Statement in the McDonald's worksheet, we would see a Δ Working Capital of $90.8 million (because in this example Accounts receivable is the only account in McDonald's Working Capital).

A positive $90.8 million means Δ Working Capital increased by $90.8 million and in so doing consumed $90.8 million in cash. Therefore, the worksheet subtracts the $90.8 million as well as the $1,678.9 million of Capex to get from the Operating Cash Flow of $4,504.7 million to the $2,662.6 million of Free Cash Flow. The semantics of Working Capital can be confusing. On the one hand, we are talking about a *negative* number—($90.8) million— for Accounts receivable in McDonald's GAAP Cash Flow but on the other hand we are saying Δ Working Capital *increased* by $90.8 million. The ($90.8) million in the GAAP Cash Flow is subtracted from Net Income to get to the Net CFO number. The same $90.8 million change, however, reflects an *increase* in the Accounts receivable balance on the McDonald's balance sheet. This is the case whether we are looking only at Accounts receivable or looking at the entire Working Capital section. Note: GAAP accounting deals with foreign currency rates one way in the income statement and a different way in the balance sheet. If the company you are working on has foreign operations, the difference between, say, the Accounts receivable balance sheet numbers at 12/31/05 and 12/31/06 is probably *not* the Accounts receivable number you see in the GAAP Cash Flow. If your company has no foreign operations, the change in the two Accounts receivable balance sheet numbers is probably the same as or very close to the GAAP Cash Flow number.

Row 38: The worksheet calculates Free Cash Flow. Note: If Free Cash Flow is negative, some of the cells below Row 38 will contain an "N/A." (Not Applicable). A negative Free Cash Flow number, like a negative Net Income number, does not lend itself to ratio, multiple, or return calculations.

Row 40: Enter the weighted average diluted shares outstanding. You will find that number at the bottom of the Income Statement, just below the number for nondiluted shares. Some companies do not include this number in the Income Statement, forcing you to spend your valuable time looking for it in the Notes.

Row 41: The worksheet calculates Free Cash Flow per share.

GAAP DATA

Rows 46–47: Exhibit 6.9 shows the GAAP section of the worksheet. Enter the numbers in Rows 46 and 47. We used McDonald's Net Income from Continuing Operations number instead of their

	A	C	D	E
43				
44				
45	GAAP Data	2006	2005	2004
46	EPS	$ 2.30	$ 2.03	$ 1.79
47	Net Income	$ 2,873.0	$ 2,586.4	$ 2,277.5
48	Net Income as % of Net CFO	66%	60%	58%
49	% Δ EPS	13%	13%	
50	EPS as % of OCF per share	64%	66%	61%
51	EPS as % of FCS	108%	92%	88%

EXHIBIT 6.9 GAAP Data

Net Income number. The former number reflects the spin off of McDonald's Chipotle Mexican fast food operation.

Row 48: The worksheet calculates Net Income as a percentage of Net CFO (Cash provided by operating activities). If a company has a Net Loss or negative Net CFO, a "N/A" will appear.

Rows 49–51: The worksheet calculates these ratios so we can track the relationship between EPS and cash flow metrics. Divergent trends between EPS and FCS may offer opportunities for the Free Cash Flow investor. The trend in Row 51, from 88 percent to 108 percent, may be a sign for investors to dig deeper into McDonald's numbers.

PERCENTAGES

Rows 54–60: Exhibit 6.10 contains the Percentages section. The worksheet calculates the percentage change ("% Δ") from year to year in these metrics. This comparison enables the investor to quickly see how much each of the different components of Free Cash Flow per share (FCS) is changing so as to better understand the causes of the change in FCS.

Rows 61–63: The worksheet calculates the Operating Cash Flow Margin (OCF Margin), Capex as a percentage of Revenues, and the Free Cash Flow Margin. The trends in these percentages are critical and must be carefully watched and understood. Note that from 2005 to 2006, McDonald's Operating Cash Flow as a percent of Revenues increased slightly yet Free Cash Flow as a percent of Revenues declined. Go back to the Free Cash Flow Statement and look

	A	C	D	E
52				
53	Percentages	2006	2005	2004
54	% Δ Revenues	9%	7%	
55	% Δ Cash Operating Costs	7%	7%	
56	% Δ Operating Cash Flow	15%	6%	
57	% Δ Capex	10%	15%	
58	% Δ Free Cash Flow	−5%	9%	
59	% Δ in # of diluted shares	−2%	0%	
60	% Δ FCS	−4%	9%	
61	OCF Margin (OCF as % of Revenues)	21%	20%	20%
62	Capex as % of Revenues	8%	8%	7%
63	FCF Margin (FCF as % of Revenues)	12%	14%	14%

EXHIBIT 6.10   Percentages

at Row 36: Δ Working Capital. In both 2004 and 2005, Δ Working Capital was a source of cash, but in 2006 Δ Working Capital was a use of cash. So the Δ Working Capital shift from a "$412.3" million *source* of cash in 2005 to a $163.2 million *use* of cash in 2006 reduced the 2006 Free Cash Flow number by $575.5 million compared with the 2005 Free Cash Flow number. This is a good example why Δ Working Capital is separated from cash costs in the Free Cash Flow Statement. McDonald's has relatively low Working Capital. Companies with large Working Capital positions and large changes in Working Capital from period to period can have Net CFO numbers that are heavily influenced by Δ Working Capital. Many Wall Street analysts include changes in Working Capital in their Operating Cash Flow number. But when the items that make up Δ Working Capital are buried in GAAP's "Cash provided by operating activities" section, it is easy to miss the net impact of the Working Capital changes on the Net CFO number.

PER SHARE DATA

Rows 66–70: The worksheet calculates the per share data in Exhibit 6.11. Per share data is useful because that is what we are buying and selling: shares. Per share data—when extended to the entire Free Cash Flow chain as we have done here—helps us to better appreciate the relative importance of the different components of Free Cash Flow.

	A	C	D	E
64				
65	Per Share Data	2006	2005	2004
66	Revenues	$ 17.25	$ 15.56	$ 14.60
67	Cash Operating Costs	13.65	12.48	11.68
68	Operating Cash Flow	3.60	3.08	2.92
69	Capex	1.34	1.20	1.04
70	Free Cash Flow	$ 2.13	$ 2.21	$ 2.03

EXHIBIT 6.11 Per Share Data

INCREMENTAL DATA AND COMPANY'S REINVESTMENT RETURN

Row 73: The Incremental Data section in Exhibit 6.12 focuses on how Revenue growth increases Operating and Free Cash Flow. If we see these numbers in a declining trend we may get an indication before the EPS investors of the bloom coming off the EPS rose. Here is the formula for the 2006 number in Cell C73:

$$\text{Incremental OCF per \$1 of Additional Revenue}$$
$$= \frac{2006 \text{ OCF} - 2005 \text{ OCF}}{2006 \text{ Revenues} - 2005 \text{ Revenues}} = \$0.33 \qquad (6.1)$$

For every additional dollar of Revenue, McDonald's generated an incremental $0.33 of Operating Cash Flow.

	A	C	D	E
70	Free Cash Flow	$ 2.13	$ 2.21	$ 2.03
71				
72	Incremental Data	2006	2005	
73	Incremental OCF per $1 of additional Rev.	$ 0.33	$ 0.17	
74	Incremental FCF per $1 of additional Rev.	N/A	$ 0.19	
75				
76	Company's Reinvestment Return	2006	2005	
77	Incremental OCF	$ 580.0	$ 211.4	
78	Reinvestment (Δ WC + Capex)	1,842.1	1,110.5	
79	Reinvestment Return	31%	19%	
80	Reinvestment Return on Prior Year's Capex	34%	23%	

EXHIBIT 6.12 Incremental Data and Company's Reinvestment Return

Row 74: This is computed in the same manner as Row 73. Because McDonald's Free Cash Flow declined from 2005 to 2006, Cell C74 contains an "N/A."

Row 77: This is the only section in the worksheet that addresses the *company's* return—not *investor* return. The worksheet inputs the difference between Operating Cash Flow in the current period and that in the prior period. The cell will have an "N/A" if Operating Cash Flow declined from the prior period.

Row 78: The worksheet sums the current period's Δ Working Capital and Capex.

Row 79: The formula is:

$$\text{Reinvestment Return} = \frac{\text{Incremental OCF}}{(\Delta \text{ Working Capital} + \text{Capex})} \qquad (6.2)$$

If this number is in a declining trend, we need to understand the causes and decide whether the company is likely to turn things around.

Row 80: This is the same formula as Row 79 but it uses the *prior* year's Capex number instead of the current year's Capex number. Some Capex projects take a year or so to complete and contribute to Revenues. The longer a company's Capex projects take to be completed, the more value there may be in calculating *current* period Operating Cash Flow against *prior* period Capex. McDonald's computes one-year and three-year Reinvestment Returns (defined differently) using quarterly data. Take a look at McDonald's ROIIC and weighting disclosures in the company's 2006 annual report (they are in Appendixes D and E). It would be great for investors if all public companies provided this kind of insight into capital utilization.

CASH SOURCES AND DEPLOYMENTS

Row 82: Exhibit 6.13 begins the Cash Sources and Cash Deployment section of the worksheet. This section serves two purposes: It helps us focus on the major sources and uses of cash and it will help us project 2007 Free Cash Flow per share, deployment, and investor return. *Reminder: All of the numbers you enter from this point until the end of the worksheet must be entered as positive numbers, even if some of them appear as negative numbers in the GAAP Cash Flow.*

	A	C	D	E
82	CASH SOURCES AND CASH DEPLOYMENTS			
83	CASH SOURCES	2006	2005	2004
84	Free Cash Flow	$ 2,662.6	$ 2,814.2	$ 2,582.3
85	Sale of assets	597.4	259.1	306.3
86	Borrowings	36.4	3,130.6	261.5
87	Stock options exercised	975.7	768.1	580.5
88				
89				
90				
91				
92	Total Cash Sources	$ 4,272.1	$ 6,972.0	$ 3,730.6
93				
94	FCF as a % of Total Cash Sources	62%	40%	69%

EXHIBIT 6.13   Cash Sources

Row 84: The worksheet enters Free Cash Flow.

Rows 85–90: In these Rows we enter the major sources of cash that appear in the Investing and Financing parts of the company's GAAP Cash Flow Statement. For more examples of various items that go here, look at the other five companies in the Six Restaurants file. We typically do not list small "Other" items as they do not provide information we can use in doing the projection. You should list whatever you think will help your analysis. If there are more than six items for this group, net several items in one Row using Excel's addition function. This method also provides a permanent record of your calculation.

Row 92: The worksheet totals the items above it.

Row 94: The worksheet calculates this percentage. Keep in mind the change in "Cash and equivalents" is not included in Total Cash Sources. This ratio plus the list of Cash Sources provide insight into the company's cash sources. How does the mix change over time and what does that say about the company's financial strategy? Are the trends in the major components sustainable? Does Free Cash Flow play a major or minor role in the company's cash sources?

Row 96: Each of the four Deployments—Acquisitions, Buybacks, Dividends, and Debt—has its own section in the worksheet.

	A	C	D	E
94	FCF as a % of Total Cash Sources	62%	40%	69%
95				
96	CASH DEPLOYMENTS	2006	2005	2004
97	Acquisitions			
98	Acquisitions	$ 238.6	$ 343.5	$ 149.7

EXHIBIT 6.14   Acquisitions

ACQUISITIONS

Row 98: Enter the amount of cash spent on Acquisitions in each year. You will find these numbers in the Investing section of the GAAP Cash Flow. In the case of McDonald's shown in Exhibit 6.14, the company acquired restaurants from franchisees for various reasons. The same is true for the other restaurant firms with franchises. These franchise deals are not acquisitions of other companies in the conventional sense but we include them here.

BUYBACKS

Row 101: Because Buybacks are only one of many corporate transactions that affect the number of shares outstanding, in Exhibit 6.15 we use "Δ in number of shares" as the section title rather than "Buybacks."

	A	C	D	E
100				
101	Δ in # of shares	2006	2005	2004
102	Buybacks	$ 2,959.4	$ 1,202.0	$ 621.0
103	Stock price			
104	# of shares purchased			
105	Shares issued	$ 975.7	$ 768.1	$ 580.5
106	Stock price			
107	# of shares issued			
108	Net Δ in # of shares			
109	Weighted avg. shares - diluted	1,251.7	1,274.2	1,273.7
110	Δ FCS due to Δ in # of shares	$ 0.04	$ (0.00)	

EXHIBIT 6.15   Buybacks

Row 102: Enter the amount spent on buybacks. The number is in the Investing section of the GAAP Cash Flow. McDonald's call it "Treasury stock purchases."

Rows 103–104: Ignore for now.

Row 105: Enter the amount the company received from the issuance of new stock common shares. This includes the exercise of employee stock options, secondary stock issues, private equity placements, and other equity vehicles. Check the equity section in the Notes for clarification if the items in the Investing section are not worded clearly.

Rows 106–108: Ignore for now.

Row 109: The worksheet inputs the weighted average shares from Row 40.

Row 110: The worksheet calculates the impact on Free Cash Flow per share (FCS) due to the net purchasing and issuing of common stock shares. We want to isolate changes in FCS due to changes in the number of shares from changes in FCS due to the company's operations.

DIVIDENDS

Row 114: Exhibit 6.16 is the Dividends section. Enter the amounts paid in Dividends. The numbers are in the Financing section of the GAAP Cash Flow Statement.

Row 115: The worksheet enters the number of shares.

Row 116: The worksheet calculates Dividends paid per share.

	A	C	D	E
112				
113	Dividends	2006	2005	2004
114	Dividends	$ 1,216.5	$ 842.0	$ 695.0
115	Weighted avg. shares	1,251.7	1,274.2	1,273.7
116	Dividend paid per share	$ 0.97	$ 0.66	$ 0.55

EXHIBIT 6.16 Dividends

	A	C	D	E
118	(Dividends + Debt Service) as % of FCF			
119				
120	Debt	2006	2005	2004
121	Interest paid	$ 430.3	$ 390.3	$ 370.3
122	Debt Repayments	2,301.1	1,518.3	1,077.0
123	Borrowings	36.4	3,130.6	261.5
124	Total Cash Sources except Borrowings			
125	Total Cash Deployed			
126	Δ in Debt	(2,264.7)	1,612.3	(815.5)
127	Δ in Debt per share	$ (1.81)	$ 1.27	$ (0.64)

EXHIBIT 6.17   Debt

DEBT

Row 121: Exhibit 6.17 is the Debt section. Enter the cash amounts of interest paid if any. They are at the very bottom of the GAAP Cash Flow Statement. If they are not there, look in the Notes. If there is nothing in the Notes, use the interest expense number in the Income Statement. When we use the interest expense number, we add "expense" in the A121 title space.

Rows 122–123: Enter the Debt Repayments and Borrowings from the Financing section of the GAAP Cash Flow Statement. Many companies have multiple lines that belong in either of these two Rows, each representing a different type of debt. If so, use Excel's addition function in the cells in these two Rows.

Rows 124–125: Ignore for now.

Row 126: The worksheet calculates the change in total debt by netting Rows 122 and 123.

Row 127: The worksheet converts Row 126 into per-share numbers.

OPERATIONS

Row 131: The worksheet inputs the numbers in Row 131 of Exhibit 6.18.

Row 132: The worksheet calculates these numbers.

	A	C	D
		2006	2005
130	OPERATIONS		
131	Free Cash Flow per share (FCS)	$ 2.13	$ 2.21
132	Δ FCS from previous year	(0.08)	0.18
133	Less Δ FCS due to Δ in # of shares	0.04	(0.00)
134	Δ FCS due to existing operaions	(0.12)	0.18

EXHIBIT 6.18 Operations

Row 133: The worksheet inputs its Row 110 calculation of the change in Free Cash Flow per share due to the net impact of the purchase and issuance of shares.

Row 134: The worksheet calculates the Δ FCS due only to the changes in the operations of the business, excluding the impact of the change in the number of shares. The share number decline was worth an additional $0.04 per share and resulted in a 2006 FCS of $2.13. Without the decrease in the number of shares, FCS would have declined $0.12 rather than the actual decline of $0.08.

PROJECTING FREE CASH FLOW

Projecting Free Cash Flow is the fun part! We will estimate McDonald's 2007 Free Cash Flow and deployments. The worksheet will incorporate our Free Cash Flow estimate and our deployment estimates into a projection of McDonald's investor return. To project McDonald's 2007 results, the worksheet requires us to input our estimates of 11 numbers. Some companies will require a few more numbers and some a few less.

As you can see in Exhibit 6.19, we have now opened Column B, the projection Column. The Free Cash Flow Worksheet has one projection Column and three historical Columns. We provide guidance at the end of this chapter for investors who prefer to project more periods or input more historical periods. Hereafter the Row numbers **in bold** refer to cells in Column B.

Row 33: Only masochistic investors would attempt a projection of the GAAP CFO section so we skip the CFO section and start with the Free Cash Flow Statement. The 2007 Revenue estimates for all the companies in our restaurant group are the Street consensus

	A	B	C	D	E
31					
32	FREE CASH FLOW STATEMENT	2007E	2006	2005	2004
33	Revenues	$ 22,900.0	$ 21,586.4	$ 19,832.5	$ 18,594.0
34	Cash Operating Costs	18,091.0	17,081.7	15,907.8	14,880.7
35	Operating Cash Flow (OCF)	4,809.0	4,504.7	3,924.7	3,713.3
36	Δ Working Capital	13.3	163.2	(412.3)	(190.3)
37	Capex	1,900.0	1,678.9	1,522.8	1,321.3
38	Free Cash Flow (FCF)	$ 2,895.7	$ 2,662.6	$ 2,814.2	$ 2,582.3
39					
40	Weighted avg. shares - diluted	1,234.8	1,251.7	1,274.2	1,273.7
41	Free Cash Flow per share (FCS)	$ 2.35	$ 2.13	$ 2.21	$ 2.03
42	Stock price	$ 48.83			
43					
44					
45	GAAP Data	2007E	2006	2005	2004
46	EPS	$ 2.77	$ 2.30	$ 2.03	$ 1.79
47	Net Income		$ 2,873.0	$ 2,586.4	$ 2,277.5

EXHIBIT 6.19   Projecting Free Cash Flow

numbers. Investors who do not have Bloomberg or Reuters can obtain the Street consensus number from Yahoo! Finance, MSN Money, or a broker. Or, use your favorite analyst's number or your own number.

Row 34: The worksheet calculates the $18,091.0 after we estimate the Operating Cash Flow Margin in the next Row.

Row 35: To make an Operating Cash Flow estimate, we first need to decide on an Operating Cash Flow Margin (OCFM) for 2007E. We entered the margin (in this example, 0.21 for a 21 percent margin) in C35's formula (we use the Excel multiplication symbol "*" rather than the conventional "×"):

$$\text{Operating Cash Flow} = \text{Revenues} \times \text{OCFM} = B33 * 0.21 = \$4,809.0$$
$$(6.3)$$

Then the worksheet subtracts the Operating Cash Flow number from Revenues to get Operating Cash Costs. Here is where the Free Cash Flow Statement is an advantage to investors not mired down in an avalanche of

GAAP data. Look at the company's historical OCFM numbers and focus on this question: Will the 2007E OCFM be the same, higher, or lower than the 2006 OCFM number? McDonald's historical OCFM numbers have not been all over the place. Some companies' OCFM's will show a lot of volatility. When looking at a company that has gyrating OCFM numbers over three or four years, it may be difficult to understand the company's OCFM. Go on to the next company unless there are reasons to believe things are going to stabilize. If a company is expected to use large amount(s) of cash for purpose(s) other than our four deployments, be sure to incorporate the nondeployment cash outflow(s) in your estimate of the Operating Cash Flow Margin if they did not occur in the prior year. We looked at the McDonald's OCFM's for 2004 through 2006. After conducting our due diligence on McDonald's, we saw no reason to change McDonald's 2006 21 percent OCFM, so we added ".21" after the "0" in B35's formula "B33 * 0".

Row 36: The worksheet calculates the 2007 Δ Working Capital estimate by first (1) multiplying 2007E Revenues by the percentage in C29 (the Net of the receivables, inventories, and payables balances on the last (12/31/06) balance sheet as a percent of 2006 Revenues) and then (2) subtracting from (1) the 2006 Net number in C28. If you find the B36 formula lacking, replace the worksheet's formula with your own formula. If the number produced by this formula (or any formula in the worksheet) does not make sense, override the formula by entering a number that makes sense.

Row 37: Input a Capex estimate. All of the restaurant companies in our analysis provided a 2007E Capex number or range. Look in the 10-K, in a company press release announcing annual guidance or look at the Q4 quarterly conference call transcript at www.SeekingAlpha.com. Analyst reports are another source of information on Capex. We generally use the high end of a Capex guidance range to be conservative. If you are doing this exercise in midyear, look at the 10-Qs to see the cumulative Capex and how Capex has been distributed by quarter in previous years. Also review the Capex section in Chapter 4 for comments on Capex.

Row 38: The worksheet calculates Free Cash Flow.

Rows 40–41: Ignore for now. We will return to these Rows later.

Rows 42: Enter the current stock price.

Row 46: Enter in B46 the Street consensus EPS forecast or your own number.

Row 47: We do not use B47.

	A	B	C	D	E
82	CASH SOURCES AND CASH DEPLOYMENTS				
83	CASH SOURCES	2007E	2006	2005	2004
84	Free Cash Flow	$ 2,895.7	$ 2,662.6	$ 2,814.2	$ 2,582.3
85	Sale of assets	600.0	597.4	259.1	306.3
86	Borrowings		36.4	3,130.6	261.5
87	Stock options exercised	1,175.0	975.7	768.1	580.5
88					
89					
90					
91					
92	Total Cash Sources	$ 4,670.7	$ 4,272.1	$ 6,972.0	$ 3,730.6

EXHIBIT 6.20 Projecting Cash Sources

PROJECTING CASH SOURCES

Exhibit 6.20 shows the estimates for the major sources of cash in the projected period.

> **Row 85:** Our "Sale of assets" estimate is based on McDonald's prior years' numbers. It does not reflect McDonald's announced intentions to restructure their franchise operations. If a company is a habitual asset seller, management may be keen to minimize use of investors' capital.
>
> **Row 86:** We do not use B86 in projections. This Row is here only so you can see the historical numbers.
>
> **Row 87:** We cover this estimate in the "Δ in number of shares" section that follows. If shares are issued, be sure to enter the amount received here after you complete the Δ in number of shares section.
>
> **Rows 88–91:** If any other major sources of cash are expected, input those here. Look at the other five restaurant companies to see examples of other cash sources. Look at press releases and other filings for information on expected large sources of cash.
>
> **Row 92:** The worksheet adds the cash sources.

We next estimate three of the deployments: Acquisitions, Buybacks (netted with issuance of shares), and Dividends. After that, we use the fourth deployment—Debt (or really the net change in total debt)—to balance Cash Sources and Cash Deployments. Keep in mind we are only *approximating* a balance of the major cash flows (the accounting word *balance* is not really appropriate here because in accounting things either balance or they do not balance). As noted earlier, if the company is expected to use a large amount of cash for purposes other than our four deployments, you will need to include the nondeployment cash use(s) in your estimate of the Operating Cash Flow Margin. Alternatively, if the nondeployment cash use is a specific dollar amount, you have the option of including the number in Cash Sources—just be sure to enter the number as a negative number (an exception to our "Don't enter negative numbers after the Δ Working Capital section rule).

PROJECTING ACQUISITIONS

Row 98: Our 2007 estimate of $300.0 million for *cash* used for acquisitions is in B98 in Exhibit 6.21. McDonald's and the other five companies appear to have made no acquisitions of other firms in the 2004–2006 time frame. McDonald's historical Acquisition data represent their purchases of restaurants from their franchisees for a variety of reasons (retirement, poor performance, financial difficulties, and so on). Unless we find information in our due diligence about a company's acquisition plans, we eyeball recent activity in "Acquisitions" and put in a number that seems consistent with the historical numbers. We deal with IHOP's acquisition of Applebee's in Chapter 7.

Row 99: The formula in B99 is "= 1/B109." B109 is our estimate of 2007E shares outstanding that we will derive in the next section. If the company you are analyzing recently completed an acquisition, or it has announced an acquisition and you are confident the deal will close, replace the 1 in the B99 formula with your estimate of the acquired company's Free Cash Flow. The worksheet will calculate the estimated Free Cash Flow per share after we complete "Δ in the number of shares." Your Free Cash Flow estimate may need to be shaved to the extent the acquired company will contribute less than a full year of Free Cash Flow. The acquired company's

	A	B	C	D	E
94	FCF as a % of Total Cash Sources	62%	62%	40%	69%
95					
96	CASH DEPLOYMENTS	2007E	2006	2005	2004
97	Acquisitions				
98	Acquisitions	$ 300.0	$ 238.6	$ 343.5	$ 149.7
99	Acquired firm(s) projected FCS	$ 0.0			

EXHIBIT 6.21 Projecting Acquisitions

Free Cash Flow estimate reflects only one part of the acquisition's impact on the buyer's financials. If the buyer finances the acquisition with new debt, the new debt should be reflected in the Δ in Debt projection. If new stock shares are issued to pay all or part of the acquisition price, include the new shares in B107 (the number of new shares issued) in the "Δ in the number of shares" projection that follows. If the Company says they will use existing cash or marketable securities, that needs to be reflected in the Cash Sources section. The combined impact of these changes will affect investor return. If the buyer segments its operations in the Notes so that the seller's operations disappear into the buyer's aggregate financials, this projection will be the first and last look at the acquisition's impact on the company.

PROJECTING Δ IN SHARE VALUE DUE TO Δ IN THE NUMBER OF SHARES

Row 102: Exhibit 6.22 shows how we project the change in the number of shares. Enter your estimate for Buybacks, if any, in 2007E. Look at the amounts spent in previous years. If you are doing this in midyear, look at the 10-Qs to see what the company has already spent this year. Read what management says about plans for future buybacks in the CEO's letter in the 10-K, in the body of the 10-K, and in press releases. Be conservative. On page 25 of McDonald's 2006 10-K, management said they expect to allocate at least $5 billion to buybacks and dividends in the two years 2007 and 2008.

	A	B	C	D	E
100					
101	Δ in # of shares	2007E	2006	2005	2004
102	Buybacks	$ 2,000.0	$ 2,959.4	$ 1,202.0	$ 621.0
103	Stock price	$ 48.83			
104	# of shares purchased	41.0			
105	Shares issued	$ 1,175.0	$ 975.7	$ 768.1	$ 580.5
106	Stock price	$ 48.83			
107	# of shares issued	24.1			
108	Net Δ in # of shares	(16.9)			
109	Weighted avg. shares - diluted	1,234.8	1,251.7	1,274.2	1,273.7
110	Δ FCS due to Δ in # of shares	$ 0.03	$ 0.04	$ (0.00)	
111	Δ Share value due to Δ in # of shares	1.3%			

EXHIBIT 6.22 Projecting Δ in Share Value due to Δ in Number of Shares

Row 103: The worksheet enters the stock price. You can enter a higher price to be conservative (at a higher price, fewer shares will be purchased so the benefit to FCS will be lower).

Row 104: The worksheet calculates the number of shares purchased by dividing your estimate of the Buybacks, if any, by the stock price in B103.

Row 105: Enter your estimate of cash received, if any, from exercised stock options and other sources such as follow-on stock issues. The cash received from stock options is a function of the strike price of the options, employees' vesting status, and the market price. Unless the stock has deviated from recent levels, we look at trends in option exercise activity and go with the flow. This could be an easy estimate if your reading of the Notes suggests the options are likely to be under water. If you enter a number in B105, be sure to also put the number in the Cash Sources section above.

Row 106: The worksheet enters the stock price in B103. To be conservative, enter a lower price than the current price (at a lower price, more shares will be issued, so the damage to FCS will be greater).

Row 107: The worksheet calculates the number of shares issued, if any. If shares are expected to be issued for an acquisition, add those shares in B107 *after* the worksheet calculates the number of shares issued for cash, if any.

Row 108: The worksheet calculates the net of the estimates, if any, of Buyback shares purchased and shares issued.

Row 109: The worksheet calculates the 2007E total shares by netting any change in B108 against the prior year's number of shares. The worksheet takes the B109 estimate, puts it into the B41 formula and computes the 2007E Free Cash Flow per share.

Row 110: The worksheet calculates the change in 2007E FCS resulting from the estimate of the change in the number of shares. In McDonald's case, the estimated decrease of 16.9 million shares increases FCS by $0.03.

$$
\begin{aligned}
&\frac{\text{2007E FCF}}{\text{2007E Number of Shares}} - \frac{\text{2007E FCF}}{\text{2006 Number of Shares}} \\[6pt]
&= \frac{\text{B84}}{\text{B109}} - \frac{\text{B84}}{\text{C109}} \\[6pt]
&= \frac{\$2{,}895.7}{1{,}234.8} - \frac{\$2{,}895.7}{1{,}251.7} \\[6pt]
&= \$0.03
\end{aligned}
\tag{6.4}
$$

Row 111: The worksheet calculates the impact on the share value resulting from the increase of $0.03 in Free Cash Flow per share.

Δ Share Value due to Δ in Number of Shares

$$= \frac{\text{Net } \Delta \text{ in Number of Shares}^* - 1}{\text{Prior Period's Number of Shares}} = \frac{-16.9^* - 1}{1251.7} = 1.3\%$$

$$(6.5)$$

PROJECTING INVESTOR RETURN FROM DIVIDENDS

Row 114: In Exhibit 6.23, the worksheet calculates the estimated dividends, if any, by multiplying the number of shares estimate in B109 by the estimate of the dividends per share in B116.

Row 115: The worksheet inputs the B109 estimate of the shares outstanding.

Row 116: Enter your estimate of the company's 2007 dividends per share, if any, here.

Row 117: The worksheet calculates the investor return from Dividends (the Dividend Yield) by dividing the estimated 2007 annual dividend per share by the stock price. This dividend return ignores the additional return generated by reinvesting the dividends. The reinvestment benefit contributes significantly to investor return over time. Still, we have no problem with a company that is likely to generate an attractive investor return without paying dividends.

Row 118: The worksheet calculates a dividend payout ratio to highlight the amount of cushion a company has to make future dividend payments. Debt Service is the sum of our estimates for interest paid in 2007 and the company's 2007 scheduled debt principal

	A	B	C	D	E
112					
113	Dividends	2007E	2006	2005	2004
114	Dividends	$ 1,234.8	$ 1,216.5	$ 842.0	$ 695.0
115	Weighted avg. shares - diluted	1,234.8	1,251.7	1,274.2	1,273.7
116	Dividends paid per share	$ 1.00	$ 0.97	$ 0.66	$ 0.55
117	Dividend Yield	2.0%			
118	(Dividends + Debt Service) as % of FCF	57%			

EXHIBIT 6.23 Projecting Investor Return from Dividends

repayments. A common Street practice is to define the dividend payout ratio as:

$$\text{Dividend Payout Ratio} = \frac{\text{Dividends Paid}}{\text{Net Income}} \qquad (6.6)$$

This definition has two problems. First, it excludes interest and principal payments that are senior to dividends. If a company cannot make its interest and principal payments, the banks are not going to allow it to pay dividends. That is why we include interest and principal in our definition of the dividend payout ratio. Second, the Street's definition uses Net Income rather than Free Cash Flow. Net Income combines accrual allocations and cash flow, but cash dividends are paid in cash. That is why we use Free Cash Flow rather than Net Income as the ratio's denominator.

PROJECTING Δ IN SHARE VALUE DUE TO Δ IN DEBT

In Exhibit 6.24, we use Δ in Debt to balance the Total Cash Sources with the Total Deployments. Again, this is not an accounting exercise, so we are not necessarily including every dollar in the GAAP Cash Flow—just the major items. It is a good idea to mark each number in the GAAP Cash Flow after you have put it in the worksheet. Doing this will minimize omission of material items.

	A	B	C	D	E
118	(Dividends + Debt Service) as % of FCF	57%			
119					
120	Debt	2007E	2006	2005	2004
121	Interest paid	$ 401.8	$ 430.3	$ 390.3	$ 370.2
122	Debt Repayments	17.7	2,301.1	1,518.3	1,077.0
123	Borrowings		36.4	3,130.6	261.5
124	Total Cash Sources	$ 4,670.7			
125	Total Cash Deployed	3,552.5			
126	Δ in Debt	(1,135.9)	(2,264.7)	1,612.3	(815.5)
127	Δ in Debt per share	$ (0.92)	$ (1.81)	$ 1.27	$ (0.64)
128	Δ Share value due to Δ Debt per share	1.9%			

EXHIBIT 6.24 Projecting Δ in Share Value due to Δ in Debt

Row 121: Interest paid is included in our estimate of 2007 Operating Cash Flow. The worksheet separately projects Interest paid in the Δ in Debt projection in Exhibit 6.26 because the worksheet uses Interest paid to calculate our version of the Dividend Payout Ratio. The worksheet estimates McDonald's 2007 interest payments by first dividing the cash Interest paid in 2006 ($430.3 million) by the *average* of total debt as of 12/31/05 and 12/31/06. The resulting 4.7 percent was then multiplied by the debt outstanding at 12/31/06 (minus the 2007 scheduled debt repayments) to get the $401.8 million Interest paid estimate. This assumes no change in interest rates going forward. If you think interest rates will materially change and the company has substantial floating rate debt, adjust the average interest rate.

Row 122: The *historical* numbers in this Row are total debt repayments, scheduled *and* voluntary. The number in B122, however, is *only scheduled* debt repayments. Enter in B122 the amount of debt principal repayments scheduled for 2007. Go to the Notes and look for the Debt section. There you will find a debt repayment schedule with each future year's scheduled principal repayments for all debt outstanding. Believe it or not, as of 12/31/06, McDonald's had only $17.7 million in scheduled 2007 principal repayments (2008 scheduled repayments totaled $3.2 billion).

Row 123: B123 is left blank. Borrowings, if any, will be computed by the worksheet in B126.

Row 124: The worksheet inputs the same number that's in B92.

Row 125: The worksheet takes the three non-debt deployment estimates, if any—Acquisitions, Buybacks, and Dividends—and adds them in Total Cash Deployed.

Row 126: If the Total Cash Sources number in B124 exceeds the Total Cash Deployed number in B125, the worksheet applies the difference between B124 and B125 to a reduction in the Total debt balance, if any, in C30. If there is no debt balance in C30, the worksheet puts a "0" in B126. If the Total debt balance in C30 is less than the difference between B124 and B125, the worksheet essentially pays off the debt in full by putting the amount of the Total debt balance in B126.

On the other hand, if the Total Cash Deployed number in B125 exceeds the Total Cash Sources in B124, the worksheet assumes this entire cash flow shortfall is funded by new debt and therefore puts the shortfall number in B126. In doing so, the worksheet assumes the company does not fund the cash flow shortfall, in whole or in part, with any of its own cash.

In fact, some companies may have more than enough cash on hand (in Cash and equivalents and/or in Marketable securities) to fund all or a portion of a cash flow shortfall. In that case, you have the option of overriding the worksheet's B126 formula. If some or all of the cash flow shortfall can be funded by existing cash or marketable securities and still leave the company with an adequate operating cash balance, enter in B126 the amount of the cash flow shortfall funded by new debt after you have applied existing cash balances to the cash flow shortfall.

For example, if B126 initially shows an increase in Debt of $50 million *and* there is a total of $200 million in the Cash and Marketable securities accounts in the latest balance sheet *and* it appears $150 million is more than enough for operating cash, then enter a "0" in B126 to reflect the use of $50 million of existing cash to fund the cash flow shortfall.

Row 127: The worksheet divides B126 by B109, the number of estimated shares, to convert Δ in Debt to a per-share basis. Recall that when a company is sold, the seller must pay off the existing debt with the proceeds of the sale. The seller receives only the difference between the sales price and the outstanding debt balance if any. The difference is divided by the number of shares outstanding to obtain the owner's net proceeds per share. Therefore, whenever a company's debt level changes, the value of the equity investors' shares change. Sell-side analysts deduct existing total debt when they do a cash flow valuation of a company.

Row 128: The worksheet calculates Δ Share Value resulting from our estimate of Δ in Debt by multiplying the Δ in Debt per share in B127 by "−1." The −1 converts a decrease in Debt per share to a positive return number and converts an increase in Debt per share to a negative return number. Then the worksheet computes the change in share value due to the change in Debt per share by dividing B127*−1 by the stock price.

We acknowledge several deficiencies in the worksheet's Δ Debt projection. The Interest paid estimate in B121 does not incorporate the Δ Debt estimate. Likewise, the Δ Debt estimate does not specifically reflect any incremental interest resulting from any increase in total debt. If following the steps in the Debt section results in a materially misleading Δ Debt estimate, then either modify the estimate to eliminate the problem(s) or move on to the next company. In any event, if you are perplexed after your first reading of the Δ debt projection section, do not be concerned. The Δ debt projection section is easier to work with on a specific company than it is as a read-only exercise.

	A	B	C	D
130	OPERATIONS	2007E	2006	2005
131	Free Cash Flow per share (FCS)	$ 2.35	$ 2.13	$ 2.21
132	Δ FCS from previous year	0.22	(0.08)	0.18
133	Less Δ FCS due to Δ in # of shares	0.03	0.04	(0.00)
134	Δ FCS due to existing operations	0.19	(0.12)	0.18
135	Δ FCS due to acquisition(s)	0.00		
136	Δ FCS due to existing operations + acquisition(s)	0.19		
137	Δ Share value due to Δ Operations' FCS	8.8%		

EXHIBIT 6.25   Projecting Δ in Share Value from Operations

PROJECTING Δ IN SHARE VALUE FROM OPERATIONS

> **Rows 131–134:** The worksheet inputs all of these numbers in Exhibit 6.25.
>
> **Row 135:** The worksheet inputs this cell if there is an acquired company's estimated Free Cash Flow per share number in B99.
>
> **Row 136:** If there is a number in B135, the worksheet combines the estimated Free Cash Flow per share from the company's existing operations with the acquired company's FCS. Otherwise, the number in B136 is the same as that in B134.
>
> **Row 137:** The worksheet calculates the % Δ in share value due to 2007E Operations (existing operations combined with any acquired company's operations).

$$\frac{\Delta \text{ Share Value due to } \Delta \text{ Operations' FCS}}{2006 \text{ FCS}} = \frac{\text{B136}}{\text{C131}} = \frac{\$0.19}{\$2.13} = 8.8\%$$

$$(6.7)$$

GAAP DATA, PERCENTAGES, AND PER SHARE DATA

In Exhibit 6.26, the worksheet has calculated all of the 2007E GAAP data, Percentages, and Per Share Data. We can see how our 2007 estimates compare to McDonald's historical financials in these various ratios. The comparisons can help us fine-tune our projection assumptions. We can easily change any of our 2007E inputs to get a better understanding of the sensitivity of any number to our input change. The easiest way to get started in sensitivity analysis is to copy the Six Restaurants file. In the copy raise and lower the 2007 Revenue estimates and see how they affect Free Cash Flow

	A	B	C	D	E
43					
44					
45	GAAP Data	2007E	2006	2005	2004
46	EPS	$ 2.77	$ 2.30	$ 2.03	$ 1.79
47	Net Income		$ 2,873.0	$ 2,586.4	$ 2,277.5
48	Net Income as % of Net CFO		66%	60%	58%
49	% Δ EPS	20%	13%	13%	
50	EPS as % of OCF per share	71%	64%	66%	61%
51	EPS as % of FCS	118%	108%	92%	88%
52					
53	Percentages	2007E	2006	2005	2004
54	% Δ Revenues	6%	9%	7%	
55	% Δ Cash Operating Costs	6%	7%	7%	
56	% Δ Operating Cash Flow	7%	15%	6%	
57	% Δ Capex	13%	10%	15%	
58	% Δ Free Cash Flow	9%	−5%	9%	
59	% Δ in # of diluted shares	−1%	−2%	0%	
60	% Δ FCS	10%	−4%	9%	
61	OCF Margin (OCF as % of Revenues)	21%	21%	20%	20%
62	Capex as % of Revenues	8%	8%	8%	7%
63	FCF Margin (FCF as % of Revenues)	13%	12%	14%	14%
64					
65	Per Share Data	2007E	2006	2005	2004
66	Revenues	$ 18.55	$ 17.25	$ 15.56	$ 14.60
67	Cash Operating Costs	14.65	13.65	12.48	11.68
68	Operating Cash Flow	3.89	3.60	3.08	2.92
69	Capex	1.54	1.34	1.20	1.04
70	Free Cash Flow	$ 2.35	$ 2.13	$ 2.21	$ 2.03

EXHIBIT 6.26 GAAP Data, Percentages, and Per Share Data

and other metrics. Do the same with the OCFM, Capex, and other metrics. See how differently each company reacts to the same changes. Be sure to try out this powerful capability early on with your own companies.

INCREMENTAL DATA AND COMPANY'S REINVESTMENT RETURN

The worksheet calculates all of the 2007E numbers in Exhibit 6.27. Compare the projected numbers to the historical numbers. If there is a trend, does it bode well for the company and its investors?

	A	B	C	D
70	Free Cash Flow	$ 2.35	$ 2.13	$ 2.21
71				
72	Incremental Data	2007E	2006	2005
73	Incremental OCF per $1 of additional Rev.	$ 0.23	$ 0.33	$ 0.17
74	Incremental FCF per $1 of additional Rev.	$ 0.18	N/A	$ 0.19
75				
76	Company's Reinvestment Return	2007E	2006	2005
77	Incremental OCF	$ 304.3	$ 580.0	$ 211.4
78	Reinvestment (Δ WC + Capex)	1,913.3	1,842.1	1,110.5
79	Reinvestment Return	16%	31%	19%
80	Reinvestment Return on Prior Year's Capex	18%	34%	23%

EXHIBIT 6.27   Incremental Data and Company's Reinvestment Return

INVESTOR RETURN PROJECTION

Row 145: In Exhibit 6.28, the worksheet adds all of the return components in B141 to B144 to get the Total Investor Return projection.
Total Investor Return is the expected return from owning shares of
McDonald's stock in the projected period *assuming:*
1. Our McDonald's worksheet projections are met or exceeded by
   McDonald's actual future results and disclosures, and
2. At the end of the one-year projection period (2007E), the market
   believes McDonald's performance in the following year (2008)
   will improve relative to 2007 at least to the same extent that
   2007 performance improved over 2006 performance, and
3. McDonald's Free Cash Flow Yield does not materially change
   in the period because of changes in the market's view of the
   restaurant industry's prospects or the market's view of future
   interest rates.

	A	B
139	INVESTOR RETURN	2007E
140	Stock price	$ 48.83
141	Δ Share value due to Δ in # of shares	1.3%
142	Dividend Yield	2.0%
143	Δ Share value due to Δ Debt per share	1.9%
144	Δ Share value due to Δ Operations' FCS	8.8%
145	Total Investor Return	14.1%
146	Target price	$ 54.70

EXHIBIT 6.28   Investor Return Projection

Successful equity investing is a lot like running the high hurdles. Three hurdles must be overcome to obtain our estimated investor return with McDonald's or any company's stock. First, our projections of McDonald's Free Cash Flow and deployments must be essentially accurate. That's not easy to do, stock after stock after stock, year after year after year. Second, our Target Price must be supported by the market's view a year from now that McDonald's future will be as bright or brighter than the market's current view of McDonald's future. If we sell McDonald's stock a year from now at about $54, it will be to a buyer who believes McDonald's will continue on its current trajectory. Third, McDonald's Free Cash Flow Yield can change for reasons that have little direct relationship to McDonald's performance. For example, the market often overreacts to negative changes in perceptions of an industry's future by punishing the stocks of all companies in the industry. While there are frequently significant differences in how much each company is affected, many investors, rather than taking the time to figure out company-specific impacts, bail out of or significantly reduce their holdings in the industry. McDonald's could exceed our projection, but if the market decides the restaurant industry is headed for bad times and deserts all restaurant stocks, McDonald's stock price could fall and Investor Return would not materialize as expected. Changes in market interest rates can also affect McDonald's Free Cash Flow Yield and investor return. If interest rates increase, the market will lower equity valuations because the same Free Cash Flow will be worth less in a higher interest rate, higher-inflation economy. Again, even if McDonald's exceeds our projection, we may not be able to realize expected investor return if an interest-rate-driven decline in market valuations overwhelms McDonald's increased Free Cash Flow and share value-enhancing deployments. Of course, this dynamic works both ways. A decline in interest rates can rescue an overly optimistic Free Cash Flow/ deployments projection.

> **Row 146:** The worksheet applies a 12.1 percent increase (a 14.1 percent Total Investor Return *minus* the 2 percent Dividend Yield) to the current $48.83 stock price to get the Target stock price. If our estimates of share value are eventually reflected in the stock price, we could sell McDonald's at $54.70 and also have the dividends at $1 per share.

All calculations and statements in this book exclude the return impact of commissions, taxes, and other direct and indirect transaction costs.

Because we are projecting only one year out, we are not discounting the projected numbers. We are capturing the major factors (Revenues, OCFM, Δ Working Capital, Capex, Buybacks, Acquisitions, Debt, and Dividends) that affect investor return. By focusing at a high level on relatively few data points, investor return enables the investor to focus on a company's core return-driving variables. In doing so, some important variables will invariably be missed.

RETURN MULTIPLE

We are limited to certain choices in selecting where we will invest our funds. There are bank savings accounts, CDs, Treasuries, bonds, and stocks. Real estate and alternative investments are also possibilities. All we can do is compare the alternative potential returns and their risks and decide where we are most comfortable, given the expected time frame of our investment. Some investors compare Free Cash Flow Yields to the yields of fixed-income instruments. An Internet search for "Free Cash Flow Yield" will produce a lot of comments along these lines: "Company A has a Free Cash Flow Yield of 5 percent and that compares favorably to bond rates, so we think the stock's a good value."

This analysis is valid if we are considering buying *all* the shares of Company A and want to make sure we are likely to get sufficient excess return over fixed-income investments. But if we are buying *some* of Company A's shares and we assume we will be selling those shares at some point, then we are primarily concerned with the shares' investor return during a finite period of time. Our investor return reflects both the change in the company's Free Cash Flow and its deployment impact on share value that are likely to occur during our ownership. The problem with depending on Free Cash Flow Yield alone as a basis for comparing stock returns to bond returns is that such a comparison ignores the impact of deployment of Free Cash Flow on share value. We think it makes more sense to compare fixed-income investment alternatives to a stock's estimated investor return, not to the stock's Free Cash Flow Yield.

The Return Multiple in Exhibit 6.29 is included in the Free Cash Flow Worksheet file but is not in the SixRestaurant.xls file. The interest rates in the Return Multiple section are for illustration purposes only.

> **Row 148:** Enter the number of years in your investment time horizon. This assumes the investor return is repeatable over the time horizon.
>
> **Rows 149, 151, 153, 155:** Enter the fixed income yields.
>
> **Rows 150, 152, 154, 156:** The worksheet calculates the Return Multiple by dividing the company's total investor return in B145 by the yields of each of the fixed-income investment alternatives. The

	A	B
148	RETURN MULTIPLE	10 Years
149	Treasuries	**3.0%**
150	Investor Return versus Treasuries	4.7
151	Corporate Bonds—AAA	**4.0%**
152	Investor Return versus AAA's	3.5
153	Corporate Bonds—AA	**5.0%**
154	Investor Return versus AA's	2.8
155	Corporate Bonds—A	**6.0%**
156	Investor Return versus A's	2.4

EXHIBIT 6.29   Return Multiple

question is: Are we likely to receive from McDonald's stock a sufficiently higher return above the appropriate fixed-income alternative to compensate for the additional risk of owning McDonald's stock versus, in this example, 10-Year Treasuries? To get McDonald's Return Multiple against 10-Year Treasuries, the worksheet divides our McDonald's 14.1 percent return estimate by Treasuries 10-Year yield of 3.0 percent.

$$\text{Return Multiple} = \frac{\text{Investor Return}}{\text{Treasuries' Yield}} = \frac{\text{B145}}{\text{B151}} = \frac{14.1\%}{3.0\%} = 4.7 \qquad (6.8)$$

The Return Multiple says the expected return from owning McDonald's stock over the next year is 4.7 times the expected return from owning 10-Year Treasuries. If we think McDonald's stock is roughly 3 times riskier than Treasuries, the McDonald's risk-and-return opportunity appears favorable. If, however, we think McDonald's is six times riskier than Treasuries, it looks like we should put McDonald's aside and move on to the next stock. This is a personal judgment and each investor will decide differently. Just try to be consistent from stock to stock. Make sure the risk assessment is free of wishful thinking. We can also include as return alternatives other stocks, equity benchmarks, and other types of investments. But other equity investments cannot be used *instead of* fixed-income alternatives because we would lose the benefit of the Return Multiple as a safety valve. If all stocks are overvalued in a frenzied equity bubble, comparing McDonald's investor return only to other stocks' investor returns will not give us any protection from getting very wet when the bubble bursts. The fixed-income Return Multiple is definitely not bubble-proof but it helps us think about what is happening in the overall financial markets before we buy a stock.

ADDING PERIODS TO THE WORKSHEET

Copy and paste the projection column B or H to obtain the desired number of projection periods. The following assumes you are projecting two years (Years E1 and E2). Column B is E2 and Column C is E1. Project the first year (Year E1) per the guidance provided in this chapter. To project Year E2, make the following inputs after you have projected Year E1. As with all other formulas in the Free Cash Flow Worksheet, if you are not comfortable with these formulas, do not hesitate to modify them or input numbers over the formulas.

> **Row 30:** Enter this formula in C30: $= D30 + C126$
>
> **Row 36:** Enter this formula in B36: $= (B33*D29) - (C33*D29)$
>
> **Row 42:** Enter in B42 the Target Price in C146.

Copy and paste the historical column C or I to obtain the desired number of historical periods. Then copy the formulas in the following Rows and paste into the new columns:

> **Row 49**
> **Rows 54–60**
> **Rows 72–74**
> **Rows 76–80**
> **Rows 130–134**

USING THE WORKSHEET

Personal use of the Free Cash Flow Worksheet is included in the price of the book. *Commercial use of the Free Cash Flow Worksheet without permission of the Publisher is strictly prohibited.* Please see the Copyright page at the front of the book for further information.

Chapter 7 compares six restaurant companies. The six companies all share one key attribute: each has a positive EPS in each of the three historical years and in the projected year. Because the Free Cash Flow investor has an added perspective on these six companies not enjoyed by the EPS investor (whose view is obscured by accounting fog), the Free Cash Flow investor sees many differences among the six companies—differences not revealed by a conventional EPS/PE/ROE comparison.

Six Companies

By going through the Free Cash Flow Worksheet with McDonald's, we have made a good start in using Free Cash Flow and deployments to project investor return. In Chapter 7, we look at a group of companies in the same industry to illustrate the benefits of using Free Cash Flow as one of our primary equity metrics. We will compare six restaurant companies—McDonald's, Panera Bread, Applebee's, P. F. Chang's Bistro, Cheesecake Factory, and IHOP.

In our group of six restaurant companies we have two companies that have been around seemingly forever (McDonald's and IHOP), two companies that have been around for a while (Applebee's and Cheesecake Factory) and two firms that started up fairly recently (Panera Bread and P. F. Chang's). Because McDonald's market capitalization dwarfs the combined market caps of the other five companies, some may think it makes no sense to compare five much smaller companies to the industry giant. McDonald's does have certain advantages due to scale, but size can work both ways. Our focus is on future change and how that affects investor return. That's why so many of the graphs that follow have a *percentage* calculation as the vertical axis. Why is percentage change a good way to capture investment opportunities and minimize investment headaches? Because investor return is a percentage number. Free Cash Flow investors are percentage investors.

Many of this chapter's graphs are created from the data in the SixRestaurants.xls file. Pull up the SixRestaurants.xls file if you want to see the five other companies' historical financials and our projections of their 2007E Free Cash Flow and deployments. Here's how the companies compare by size.

EXHIBIT 7.1 Revenues

	2004	2005	2006	2007E
McDonald's	$18,594,000	$19,832,500	$21,586,400	$22,900,000
Panera Bread	479,139	640,275	828,971	1,100,000
Applebee's	1,111,634	1,216,650	1,337,921	1,300,000
P. F. Chang's	706,941	809,153	937,606	1,100,000
Cheesecake Factory	969,232	1,182,053	1,315,325	1,500,000
IHOP	359,002	348,023	349,560	400,000

*(000s)

REVENUES

The six companies in Exhibit 7.1 have different business models. McDonald's, Panera, and Applebee's have both company-owned and franchise units. P.F. Chang's units and Cheesecake Factory units are all company-owned. IHOP's units are all franchises except for a few company-owned restaurants. IHOP initiated a fundamental restructuring of their business model in 2003, moving from a franchise model—in which IHOP financed the real estate and equipment for franchisees—to the current model in which the franchisees take care of their own financing. The restructuring led to lower Revenues (IHOP had Revenues of $405 million in 2003). While this book was in preparation, IHOP acquired Applebee's, conveniently providing us the opportunity to use our Free Cash Flow Statement in an acquisition analysis. In this chapter and Chapter 8 we deal with IHOP and Applebee's on a pre-merger basis except for our analysis of the merger itself.

PERCENTAGE CHANGE IN REVENUES

Exhibit 7.2 shows the percentage change in Revenues from 2005 through 2007E. Change in Revenues is the first driver of Free Cash Flow. Starting at the top left, Panera Bread is clearly in a class by itself. Any company growing Revenues by one third or so each year for three years has to be doing just about everything right—at least for the customers. Cheesecake Factory's growth rate took quite a fall but is increasing again. P.F. Chang's growth rate is way below Panera's but it is consistently higher each year. Applebee's Revenues are projected to decline in 2007 because they decided to slow unit growth (growth in the number of restaurants) in 2007. Applebee's apparently concluded it would be easier to manage a slower growth operation. McDonald's is about 20 times larger than these other

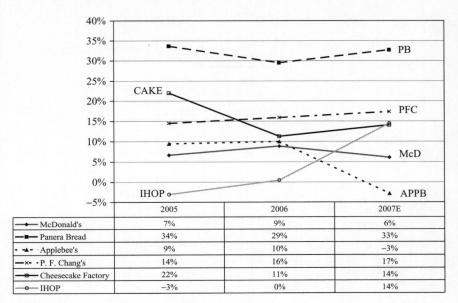

EXHIBIT 7.2 Percentage Change in Revenues

	2005	2006	2007E
McDonald's	7%	9%	6%
Panera Bread	34%	29%	33%
Applebee's	9%	10%	−3%
P. F. Chang's	14%	16%	17%
Cheesecake Factory	22%	11%	14%
IHOP	−3%	0%	14%

outfits. Setting aside Applebee's 2007E drop, McDonald's is the only single-digit Revenue growth company. The larger the company, the more difficult it usually is to produce high Revenue growth rates. IHOP's decline in 2005 reflected their fundamental restructuring of their business model that started in 2003. Except for IHOP, Revenue growth in this group by and large reflects annual increases in each chain's *number* of restaurants—*not* increased sales per restaurant. The Capex numbers will confirm the rapid expansion in units.

OPERATING CASH FLOW MARGIN

OCFM improvement is the second driver of Free Cash Flow growth. In Exhibit 7.3, McDonald's and IHOP have improved their Operating Cash Flow Margins since they initiated their new management strategies. Both of these companies' CEOs conceived and implemented fundamentally new business strategies—at some personal risk—and pulled it off. Both of these CEOs could have continued on with the strategies inherited from their respective predecessors. They may well have been able to produce minor improvements in the old business model and many people, including their

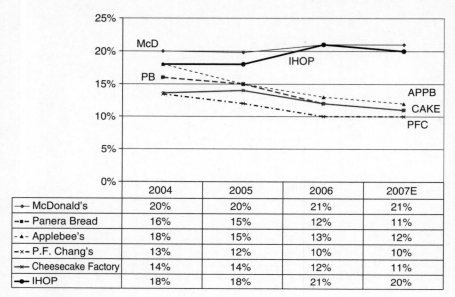

EXHIBIT 7.3   Operating Cash Flow Margin

	2004	2005	2006	2007E
—◆— McDonald's	20%	20%	21%	21%
—■— Panera Bread	16%	15%	12%	11%
-▲- Applebee's	18%	15%	13%	12%
-×- P.F. Chang's	13%	12%	10%	10%
—✳— Cheesecake Factory	14%	14%	12%	11%
—●— IHOP	18%	18%	21%	20%

directors, would not have been displeased had they done so. But they decided to make fundamental changes in the company's allocation of capital and human resources. Had these two CEOs' bold new programs fallen flat, they would have been sitting targets for internal opponents and external competitors. But had they continued their predecessors' *modus operandi,* the major improvements in their company's Operating Cash Flow Margins would never have happened.

The Operating Cash Flow Margin of above-average operators like McDonald's and IHOP is around 20 percent. What does the graph say about the other four companies? In some years they are so close together it is hard to tell them apart. Applebee's, Panera, Chang's and Cheesecake have Operating Cash Flow Margins in the vicinity of 12 percent, at least in this time period. Investors can get a faster and more comparable angle on the relative performance of companies in the same industry by using the OCFM. The OCFM includes all cash costs without interference from accrual allocations and changes in Working Capital or other balance sheet accounts. Notice how stable the OCFM is on a year-to-year basis for all of the companies. By the way, to save space, we will refer to Panera Bread, P. F. Chang's Bistro and Cheesecake Factory together as the *Three Musketeers.* Two-thirds or 12 of the 18 annual changes in the OCFM numbers are 0 percent or 1 percent. Three of the changes are 2 percent and three are 3 percent. Why do the SEC and FASB say cash flows are too volatile to be useful to investors? Perhaps they are looking at the wrong data.

Is there an ideal OCFM? Not really. Both McDonald's and IHOP have OCFMs around 20 percent. That's a good level if Capex is generally below 10 percent of Revenues. But there are many different ways to get to a positive Free Cash Flow. Some oil and gas exploration companies have OCFMs over 50 percent but have unappealing Free Cash Flow numbers because Capex as a percentage of Revenues is over 50 percent. Look for companies with positive Free Cash Flow that have improving OCFMs and the prospects for more of the same.

CAPEX AS A PERCENTAGE OF REVENUES

Think of each new restaurant as a microfactory. A restaurant's raw materials might be meat, potatoes, vegetables, and spices rather than steel, plastic pellets, or cotton. A restaurant's products are heated in kitchen ovens and blenders rather than blast furnaces and injection-molding machines. McDonald's and Applebee's are chugging along in Exhibit 7.4 with Capex

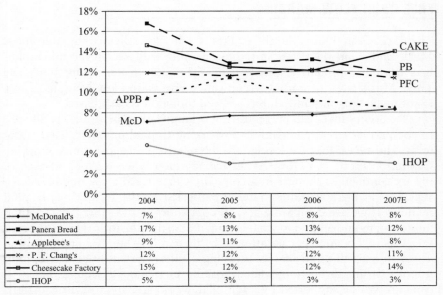

	2004	2005	2006	2007E
——♦—— McDonald's	7%	8%	8%	8%
——■—— Panera Bread	17%	13%	13%	12%
- -▲- - Applebee's	9%	11%	9%	8%
——×— · P. F. Chang's	12%	12%	12%	11%
——□—— Cheesecake Factory	15%	12%	12%	14%
——○—— IHOP	5%	3%	3%	3%

EXHIBIT 7.4 Capex as Percentage of Revenues

as a percentage of Revenues mostly under 10 percent. IHOP's all-franchise business model has virtually eliminated Capex.

With Capex/Revenue percentages between 11 percent and 17 percent, the Three Musketeers have been building new restaurants as fast as they can. The number of new restaurants opened by Panera, Chang's, and Cheesecake in 2006 as a percentage of total owned restaurants at the beginning of the year was 23 percent, 19 percent, and 24 percent, respectively. Apparently the maximum annual percentage increase in the number of restaurants a management team of a $1 billion casual dining restaurant company can handle (while keeping the existing units running smoothly) is about 20 percent to 25 percent. Cheesecake Factory's spacious restaurants make for more complex and expensive construction projects than Panera's or Chang's relatively modest sites. That may explain why Cheesecake is below the other two as measured by percentage unit increase and above the other two when measured by Capex as a percent of Revenues. What about maintenance Capex? The restaurant industry provides more Capex data than most industries. McDonald's spent over $1 billion on remodeling existing restaurants in 2006. The Three Musketeers are too new to spend much on remodeling their restaurants. At some point, however, restaurant remodeling will contribute materially to their Capex.

FREE CASH FLOW MARGIN

The Free Cash Flow Margin is Free Cash Flow divided by Revenues. McDonald's and IHOP are in the top bracket with very respectable numbers around 15 percent. Applebee's is in the middle in a declining trend. The Three Musketeers all started with positive Free Cash Flow Margins. There is not much volatility in Exhibit 7.5 even though it is cash-based.

We do not include a graph of Δ Working Capital because it is difficult to compare different companies' Δ Working Capital numbers. That is not to say, however, that we can ignore the relative impact of the Δ Working Capital on Free Cash Flow. As we will see later when we look at each of the six companies, changes in a company's Free Cash Flow numbers from year to year are sometimes materially affected by the Δ Working Capital number. If we are comparing several companies in the same industry, it is important to understand to what extent, if any, their historical and projected Free Cash Flow numbers are affected by their Δ Working Capital numbers.

Also keep in mind that Δ Working Capital can easily be a long term *use* of cash for those companies whose business models require that Revenue growth be supported by additional Working Capital. Unfortunately, Δ Working Capital is usually not a long term *source* of cash. At some point,

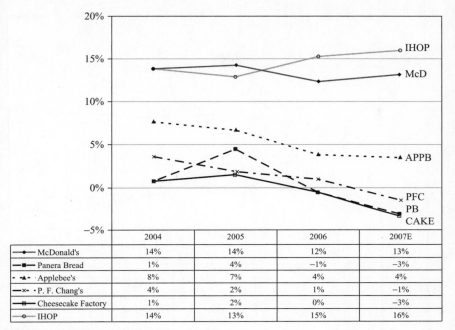

	2004	2005	2006	2007E
——◆—— McDonald's	14%	14%	12%	13%
——■—— Panera Bread	1%	4%	−1%	−3%
- -▲- · Applebee's	8%	7%	4%	4%
—×- · P. F. Chang's	4%	2%	1%	−1%
——□—— Cheesecake Factory	1%	2%	0%	−3%
——○—— IHOP	14%	13%	15%	16%

EXHIBIT 7.5 Free Cash Flow Margin

Days receivable and inventory cannot be reduced further without endangering Revenues. Days payables can be extended only so far before driving off vendors.

FREE CASH FLOW PER SHARE

Exhibit 7.6 shows McDonald's new strategy increased Free Cash Flow per share from 2004 to 2005 but saw a drop in 2006. IHOP's new business model raised FCF per share 213 percent in the same period. Applebee's FCF per share declined from 2004 to 2006. Free Cash Flow investors select stocks on the basis of (1) demonstrated ability to generate Free Cash Flow, (2) proven commitment to investor returns in the deployment of Free Cash Flow, and (3) our assessment that both (1) and (2) will continue in the future in such a way as to increase investor return. Some investors will argue that the Three Musketeers are growth stocks and therefore cannot be compared to the other three chains. These investors are willing to pay high prices for the stocks of high growth companies because they believe that at some

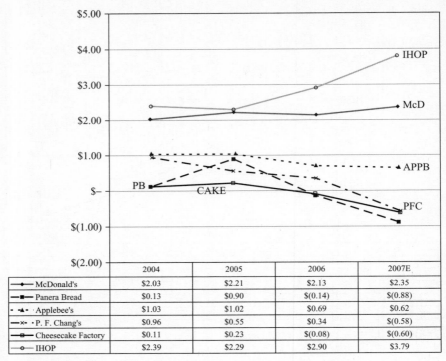

	2004	2005	2006	2007E
McDonald's	$2.03	$2.21	$2.13	$2.35
Panera Bread	$0.13	$0.90	$(0.14)	$(0.88)
Applebee's	$1.03	$1.02	$0.69	$0.62
P. F. Chang's	$0.96	$0.55	$0.34	$(0.58)
Cheesecake Factory	$0.11	$0.23	$(0.08)	$(0.60)
IHOP	$2.39	$2.29	$2.90	$3.79

EXHIBIT 7.6   Free Cash Flow per Share

point in the future the companies will be worth a lot more. But we assess companies on the basis of their expected Free Cash Flow and deployment of the Free Cash Flow. Free Cash Flow investors do not dream about the future. The Free Cash Flow investor understands that after Cheesecake runs out of Cheesecake locations in the United States, management will probably continue building Grand Lux Cafés, and when they run out of Grand Lux Café locations, they will likely focus on their new Asian concept, and when they run out of those, they may add some other new restaurant concept. Chang's already has two other brands: Pei Wei and a Taneko Japanese Tavern. Both of these companies will probably have high Capex numbers as they expand geographically and develop new restaurant brands. It is unlikely we will see a Panera Bagel 'n' Burger or a Panera Tuscan Tub 'n' Tavern. But Panera will come up with something. And who knows when one or all three companies will open restaurants in China, India, or Europe? In any event, aggressive building of new restaurants means a high level of Capex and a high level of Capex often results in little or no Free Cash Flow.

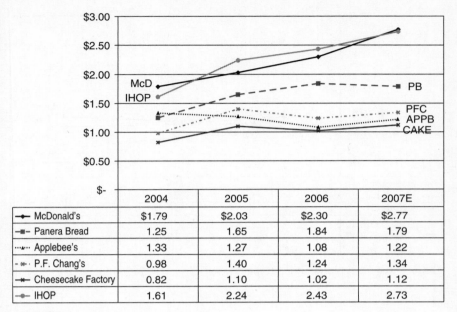

	2004	2005	2006	2007E
—◆— McDonald's	$1.79	$2.03	$2.30	$2.77
—■— Panera Bread	1.25	1.65	1.84	1.79
····▲···· Applebee's	1.33	1.27	1.08	1.22
-※- P.F. Chang's	0.98	1.40	1.24	1.34
—✳— Cheesecake Factory	0.82	1.10	1.02	1.12
—●— IHOP	1.61	2.24	2.43	2.73

EXHIBIT 7.7   The Government Number

THE GOVERNMENT NUMBER

Compared to the graphs we have seen thus far, Exhibit 7.7 presents a fundamentally different portrait of the absolute and relative performance of these six companies in the 2004-to-2007E time frame. First, all of the EPS numbers in this graph are positive. Second, with the exception of Applebee's, all of these companies are on an essentially upward EPS trend line. Earnings per share divides the group three ways. McDonald's and IHOP are in the top-earning category, Panera Bread is in the middle by itself, and the rest bring up the bottom. But the most important point about the six companies is that not one of these six companies has a negative EPS in any of these four years. GAAP would have investors believe that all six companies are doing great things for investors.

NET NONWORKING CAPITAL ITEMS

What is "Net Nonworking Capital Items in CFO as a percent of Net Income"? Recall that we removed the Working Capital and other balance

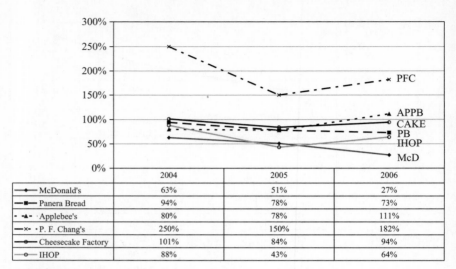

	2004	2005	2006
——◆—— McDonald's	63%	51%	27%
——■—— Panera Bread	94%	78%	73%
- -▲- - Applebee's	80%	78%	111%
——×- - P. F. Chang's	250%	150%	182%
——●—— Cheesecake Factory	101%	84%	94%
——○—— IHOP	88%	43%	64%

EXHIBIT 7.8 Net Nonworking Capital Items

sheet items from the Cash From Operations (CFO) section of the GAAP Cash Flow Statement to get to our definition of Operating Cash Flow. Having removed those items, we then net all of the remaining "Charges and credits" adjustment items in the CFO section. The percentage data in this graph represent the *net* of all the Charges and credit items *divided by* Net Income. Exhibit 7.8 suggests that accounting accrual allocations—and the judgments, estimates, and guesses that go into their calculations—can have *in the aggregate* a fairly significant effect on Net Income and EPS numbers.

In Exhibit 7.8 we see the same company groupings as we see in many of the other graphs. The differences are primarily due to the size of the depreciation charge relative to Net Income as well as to the differences in the six companies' business models. P. F. Chang's relatively high numbers mostly reflect the company's equity-linked employee compensation structure. This graph suggests we should not get too excited about EPS numbers one way or the other. A massive amount of opinion and judgment go into each EPS number. Every time there is a news story about a company that is experiencing problems with its accounting practices (and therefore its EPS numbers), we are learning about problems with accruals, allocations, and other noncash issues. That is because accrual accounting forces management to make estimates and judgments that *are often hard to make.* Have you ever seen a news story about a company miscounting its cash receipts or disbursements and having to restate its financials?

We are not suggesting that accrual accounting should be replaced by cash books. But if the SEC were to require public companies to provide a cash receipts and disbursements statement in addition to the current accrual statements, investors would have a much clearer idea of public companies' financial performance. The SEC should also require a new line in the Income Statement that indicates the net impact the changes in accrual allocations had on Net Income and EPS. In the meantime, the more other investors focus on EPS, the more good investment opportunities there are for Free Cash Flow investors.

We do not want to ignore EPS because the difference between EPS and FCS creates an advantage for Free Cash Flow investors that we can exploit to increase our returns. Now we are going to take a quick look at the six companies one by one. The first company, McDonald's, is a good example of how the differences between EPS and FCS can sometimes create opportunities for Free Cash Flow investors.

MCDONALD'S

At first glance, Exhibit 7.9 might seem to suggest Free Cash Flow per share offers no material value added over EPS, at least for McDonald's in this

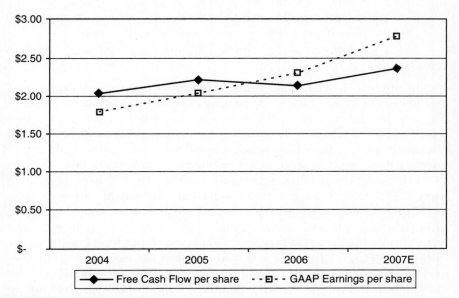

EXHIBIT 7.9 McDonald's

time period. We couldn't disagree more. There is a material difference in the trend line between FCS and EPS. Not only did FCS start higher and end lower than EPS, but look also at the respective differences between the 2004 numbers and the 2007E numbers. EPS is taking off in this period while FCS is stumbling upward. Fortunately, management appears to be aware of the need to increase Free Cash Flow. In the 2006 Annual Report, McDonald's management makes it clear they are willing to incur significant book losses in the next several years from a new restructuring program. The new initiative is composed of two parts: (1) conversion of company-owned restaurants in the U.K. and Canada to franchises so as to get under a 30 percent target for company-owned as a percentage of total restaurants and (2) conversion of 2,300 primarily company-owned restaurants in Latin America, Asia Pacific, Middle East, and Africa to franchises that are financially independent of McDonald's. In (2), McDonald's receives a royalty based on a percentage of sales but invests none of its capital in the franchise. McDonald's' initiative does not appear to be dissimilar from IHOP's restructuring program. Perhaps McDonald's liked what it saw in IHOP's turnaround? Anyway, here is what McDonald's 2006 Annual Report says about the 2,300 restaurants they want to convert:

> *The 2,300 restaurants ... represented nearly $3 billion in sales in 2006, but only generated $30 million in operating income after impairment and other charges. To achieve these results, we spent about $180 million in selling, general and administrative expenses and invested more than $100 million in capital expenditures.*[1]

In other words, McDonald's looks at Revenues, margins, and capital utilization as the three drivers of the company's financial performance. Where have we heard that before? McDonald's restaurant conversions should improve margins and reduce Capex going forward. Revenues will be affected negatively but Free Cash Flow should benefit. Some companies would never sacrifice Revenues in order to raise margins and reduce capital use.

Free Cash Flow per share helps us see McDonald's challenges are greater than its EPS numbers suggest. It should be noted McDonald's is more leveraged with debt than any of the other five companies. Looking forward, debt reduction represents one more option the company has to increase investor return. And the best part is yet to come for Free Cash Flow investors focused on FCS. McDonald's wants to complete these conversions by the end of 2008. Management says they will not be able to recover $800 million in historical currency translation losses or most of the $2.2 billion net book value of the restaurants. They expect the resulting book loss will be "significant."[2] Will McDonald's massive book losses ravage its EPS and scare away some EPS investors? If so, the drop in the stock price may create an opportunity for Free Cash Flow investors. If we like the prospects for the rest of the business, we may be able to buy the stock as the book losses hit the stock price. We can then ride the stock up as Free Cash Flow per share rapidly increases before EPS recovers. When it works, it is called "exploiting the Government Number."

PANERA BREAD

There are material differences between Panera Bread's FCS and EPS numbers, as shown in Exhibit 7.10. The EPS numbers are significantly higher and the trend lines are different. Revenues in 2006 were up 29 percent over 2005, enabling Panera to increase EPS in spite of a decline in its GAAP operating profit margin from 13 percent in 2005 to 11 percent in 2006. Panera's Free Cash Flow Statement shows its Operating Cash Flow Margin decreased from 15 percent to 12 percent. Panera's Depreciation expense increased 34 percent from 2005 to 2006, while its Capex increased 33 percent. Capex as a percentage of Revenues was 13 percent in both years. The decrease in the Free Cash Flow per share was caused partly by the continued Capex spending in spite of the OCFM decline. But a major factor was the Δ Working Capital in 2006 being a much smaller source of cash than it was in 2005. In 2005, the increase in accrued expenses was a $26.4 million source of cash. In 2006, however, accrued expenses were only a $7.6 million source of

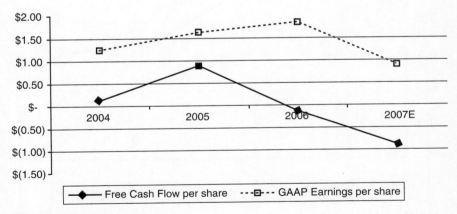

EXHIBIT 7.10 Panera Bread

cash. The Notes reveal the three largest components of accrued expenses are capital expenditures, unredeemed gift cards, and compensation and related employment taxes. The impact of Δ Working Capital on the 2005–2006 EPS-FCS comparison is a good example of one of the challenges facing non-CPA Free Cash Flow investors. From time to time, the use of Free Cash Flow will result in what is called "The Opaque Accounting Syndrome Thicket" or "TOAST" for short. When we find ourselves lost in the thicket, we have two escape options: We can solicit assistance from a CPA or otherwise equally gifted practitioner of the accounting craft, or we can move on to the next stock.

APPLEBEE'S

As shown in Exhibit 7.11, Applebee's had *some* Free Cash Flow before it was acquired by IHOP. How did Applebee's get itself into a position where it was acquired by a much smaller company? The 2006 Annual Report makes it clear that management is not happy with where the company is not going. Nowhere in the Annual Report do we find the CEO's vision of the future

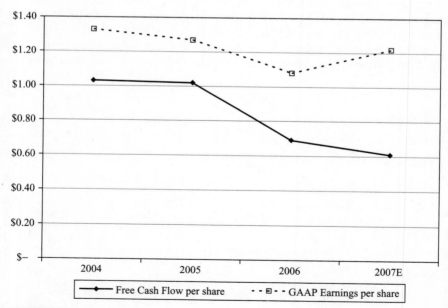

EXHIBIT 7.11 Applebee's

that integrates a strong restaurant operation (from the point of view of the satisfied customer) with strong financial performance (from the point of view of the satisfied investor). That integration is an important responsibility of the CEO. Is perfect execution necessary? No, effective execution will do the trick. If the CEO cannot make it happen, no one can.

P. F. CHANG'S BISTRO

Exhibit 7.12 has the Chang's FCS and EPS numbers and estimates. Revenues increased 16 percent from 2005 to 2006. Chang's GAAP operating profit margin declined from 7.6 percent in 2005 to 5.7 percent in 2006. Depreciation expense was unchanged as a percentage of Revenues: 4.6 percent in 2005 and 4.8 percent in 2006. The OCFM decreased from 12 percent to 10 percent. Capex as a percentage of Revenues was 12 percent in both 2005 and 2006. As with Panera, the Δ Working Capital was a major contributor to the difference between the 2005 and 2006 FCS number. Unlike Panera, however, the Δ Working Capital enabled Chang's to have a positive Free Cash Flow in 2006. Chang's had a 2006 Δ Working Capital of ($27.4)

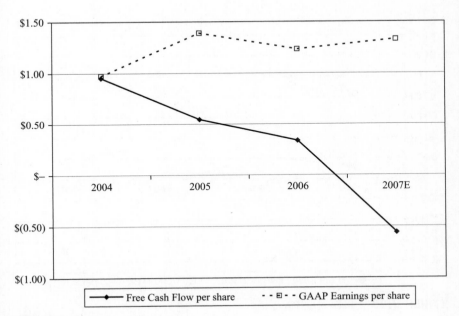

EXHIBIT 7.12 P. F. Chang's Bistro

million (Δ Working Capital was a source of $27.4 million in cash flow). But Chang's 2006 Free Cash Flow was only $9.1 million, so if Δ Working Capital had been $0, Free Cash Flow per share would have been ($0.68) in 2006, not $0.34. The 2005–2006 changes in accrued expenses and in lease obligations were two of the largest causes for the large 2006 Δ Working Capital. This is another example of why it is useful to remove the Δ Working Capital items from GAAP's Net Cash from Operations. Investors who use the Free Cash Flow Statement always know *how much* and *in which direction* the Δ Working Capital affects Free Cash Flow. Investors who do not use the Free Cash Flow Statement can easily misinterpret both increases and decreases in annual Free Cash Flow and trends.

CHEESECAKE FACTORY

Exhibit 7.13 has Cheesecake Factory's FCS and EPS numbers and estimates. Revenues grew 11 percent in 2006 over 2005. Its GAAP operating income margin declined from 11 percent in 2005 to 8 percent in 2006. Depreciation as a percentage of Revenues was 4 percent in 2005 and also 4 percent in 2006. The OCFM was 14 percent in 2005 and 12 percent in 2006. Capex

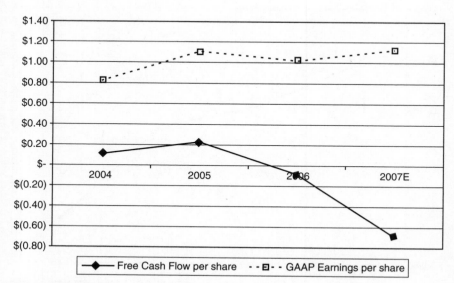

EXHIBIT 7.13   Cheesecake Factory

as a percentage of Revenues was 12 percent in both 2005 and in 2006. The Δ Working Capital numbers—($3.5) million in 2005 and $4.8 million in 2006—were not really large enough to affect each year's result but the *swing* in Δ Working Capital from a source of cash in 2005 to a use of cash in 2006 was enough to take Cheesecake into negative Free Cash Flow in 2006. In 2007 Cheesecake Factory used new debt to finance $200 million in stock buybacks. The stock buybacks resulted in remaining investors owning a larger share of the company's negative Free Cash Flow. We are pleased to refer to Cheesecake's press release on its Q3 2007 results. The Q3 release announced a reduction in the company's plan for new restaurant openings for 2008 compared to 2007. This Capex reduction may represent a shift in Cheesecake Factory's corporate financial strategy. Here is a quote from Cheesecake's October 23, 2007 press release:

Fiscal 2008 Growth Plan
The Company also announced its preliminary growth plan for fiscal 2008, which is aimed at continued expansion of its concepts in high-quality locations, returning cash to stockholders through share repurchases and managing its business to drive improvement in the Company's operating income margin.

The Company plans to open as many as 17 new restaurants in fiscal 2008 consisting of as many as 12 to 13 Cheesecake Factory restaurants, three to four Grand Lux Cafés and one Rock Sugar Pan Asian Kitchen, the Company's newest concept.

As a result of this plan, the Company's goal is to achieve the following key objectives:

- *Capitalizing on a full pipeline of premier locations to achieve its development target in fiscal 2008 while simultaneously positioning the Company to smooth out its new restaurant opening schedule in fiscal 2009 and beyond. This is intended to reduce the heavy concentration of openings in the second half of the year;*
- *Reducing total cash capital expenditures in fiscal 2008 by approximately 20 percent to an estimated range of $160 million to $170 million. The reduction will come from building fewer new restaurants and also from building more efficient, less capital intensive Grand Lux Cafés. The Company believes this will enable it to generate free cash flow of approximately $60 million to $70 million, which it expects to employ in*

support of share repurchases under its existing 4.7 million-share repurchase authorization; and

- *Improvement in the Company's operating income margin of approximately 30 to 50 basis points in fiscal 2008 as a result of lower preopening costs and increased leverage of general and administrative (G&A) expenses.*

"Our plan for fiscal 2008 contains both operational and financial advantages that are intended to benefit the Company and our stockholders for the next several years," continued Overton. "We will continue our growth next year through the addition of 17 new restaurants and also establish the foundation to open new restaurants at a more even pace throughout the year, beginning in fiscal 2009. This effort further reinforces the strong growth plan we have in place for The Cheesecake Factory, anchored by the previously identified 60 to 70 high-quality locations of the size and scope we are building today. We are meeting a number of objectives that we established for ourselves with this plan, including lowering our capital investment costs for Grand Lux Café, continuing to actively repurchase shares and improving our operating margins," concluded Overton.[3]

Cheesecake's CEO, David Overton is a genius at building and running restaurants. If he has decided to place a higher long term priority on Free Cash Flow per share and sound deployment than on EPS, his company's investors should benefit.

IHOP

The graph in Exhibit 7.14 indicates that a Free Cash Flow investor may have had an edge over an EPS investor in the several years leading up to IHOP's announcement of the Applebee's deal. FCS was increasing rather nicely with EPS lagging behind. This kind of trend differential is when Free Cash Flow investors like to strike, buying a stock before EPS investors know what's happening.

Now is a good time to look at IHOP's acquisition of Applebee's. We put together the worksheet in Exhibit 7.15 to get a handle on how the $2.1 billion all-cash acquisition affects IHOP's investors. Because we are using only cash numbers, our Operating Cash Flow Margin helps us quickly combine the two companies' operations.

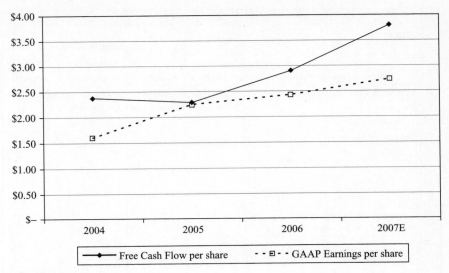

EXHIBIT 7.14 IHOP

Look at the Revenues and Free Cash Flow numbers of IHOP and Applebee's in Columns BC and BD. Applebee's Revenues are more than three times IHOP's yet IHOP's Free Cash Flow is 15 percent higher than Applebee's. If IHOP can transform Applebee's "Free Cash Flow as a percent of Revenues" to IHOP's level and keep the customers and franchisees happy, will IHOP's investors benefit? We have combined the two companies' 2007E numbers in column BE. Let's assume a *best case* scenario. If the results look anything less than stellar, we will know there's no point in spending more time on this deal. We will assume IHOP management can do to Applebee's what IHOP management did to IHOP (IHOP's Free Cash Flow rose 46 percent in the 2005–2007E period). So the $135 million in cell BF32 represents IHOP's 2007E Free Cash Flow *plus* Applebee's 2007E Free Cash Flow *plus* a 50 percent increase in Applebee's 2007E Free Cash Flow.

IHOP is taking on $2 billion in debt to do the deal. IHOP expects to generate $950 million in cash from IHOP's restructuring of Applebee's, of which about $550 million comes from the conversion of Applebee's company-owned restaurants to franchises and about $400 million is generated by the sale and leaseback of restaurant real estate. The net of the $2 billion new debt and the $950 million restructuring proceeds is the $1.05 billion in cell BF41. We have generously ignored interest expense on the new debt. If all of the $135 million combined Free Cash Flow were used

	BB	BC	BD	BE	BF
22					
23				IHOP +	
24				Applebee's	2008E
25	(000's) except per share data	IHOP	Applebee's	Combined	Combined
26	**Free Cash Flow Statement**	2007E	2007E	2007E	Adjusted*
27	Revenues	$ 400,000	$ 1,300,000	$ 1,700,000	
28	Cash Operating Costs	320,000	1,144,000	1,464,000	
29	Operating Cash Flow	80,000	156,000	236,000	
30	Δ Working Capital	4,513	(455)	4,058	
31	Capex	10,000	110,000	120,000	
32	Free Cash Flow	$ 65,487	$ 46,455	$ 111,942	$ 135,170
33					
34	Number of shares outstanding	17,265	17,265	17,265	17,265
35	Free Cash Flow per share (FCS)	$ 3.79	$ 2.69	$ 6.48	$ 7.83
36	New debt				$ 2,000,000
37	New debt per share				$ 115.84
38	Proceeds from sale of company units				$ 550,000
39	Proceeds from sale/leasebacks				$ 400,000
40					
41	Net new debt after asset sales				$ 1,050,000
42	Net new debt per share				$ 60.82
43					
44	Years required for Combined Adjusted Free Cash Flow to pay off Net New Debt				7.8
45	* Excludes tax benefits				

EXHIBIT 7.15   IHOP's Acquisition of Applebee's

to repay the $1.05 billion debt, IHOP would repay all of the debt in eight years. IHOP will not likely be paying dividends or doing buybacks at any meaningful levels for at least several years. If they did, the debt will remain longer than eight years. Big picture, we have been exceedingly generous in our assumptions. It is hard to see how the integration of the two companies could go any better than this for IHOP. Of course, IHOP will not have to repay all debt to pay some dividends or do buybacks. But even assuming a best case scenario, it looks like IHOP is taking on a huge debt load that will overhang the transition period. This debt load plus uncertainty about the pace and benefits of IHOP's restructuring of Applebee's may dominate the stock for a long time to come. It is way too soon, therefore, to say whether the Applebee's acquisition will be a good deal for IHOP investors.

Was the $25 a share a good deal for Applebee's investors? In agreeing to the $25 share price, a majority of Applebee's Board of Directors were essentially saying they had no confidence in management's ability to improve the company's long-term performance. They also had no confidence in their own ability as a Board to find a new CEO to improve the company's long-term performance. What the Applebee's Board needed was a CEO with proven turnaround experience in the restaurant industry. And that is exactly what they got; an experienced, successful restaurant industry CEO knocked on their door and gave them a PowerPoint presentation. Yet the Applebee's Board apparently did not extend a job offer to Julia Stewart, IHOP's CEO, to abandon IHOP, become Applebee's CEO, turnaround Applebee's, and take its stock to $50. Instead, the Applebee's board said to Ms. Stewart: "We think $25 a share and you as CEO of IHOP/Applebee's is a great deal for Applebee's investors. That sure beats your becoming CEO of Applebee's and moving our stock to $50!" Then again, perhaps the Applebee's Board asked Julia Stewart to be Applebee's CEO and Ms. Stewart turned them down. We have no idea what transpired in the discussions leading up to the deal's announcement but here is a simple question. Which would you prefer: turning around Applebee's as CEO of Applebee's only, with $180 million of debt or turning around Applebee's as CEO of IHOP/Applebee's, with $1 billion of debt?

THREE MUSKETEERS WITHOUT NEW UNIT CAPEX

What would the Three Musketeers' Free Cash Flow per share numbers look like if they did not build *any* new restaurants? The graph in Exhibit 7.16 removes all new restaurant Capex from total company Capex and new restaurant pre-opening costs from total Cash Operating Costs in the 2007E Free Cash Flow calculations of Panera, Chang's, and Cheesecake. We also reduced the Three Musketeers' 2007E Revenues proportionally. The McDonald's, Applebee's, and IHOP 2007E numbers are unchanged. To be sure, it makes no sense for any of the Three Musketeers to completely shut down new restaurant openings. This graph suggests, however, that all three firms could generate substantial Free Cash Flow by reducing new restaurant Capex.

WHOSE RETURN ON EQUITY?

Let's take another look, in Exhibit 7.17, at one of the Street's favorite ratios: Return on Equity (ROE). ROE is calculated this way:

$$\text{Return on Equity} = \frac{\text{Net Income}}{\text{Shareholders' Equity}} \qquad (7.1)$$

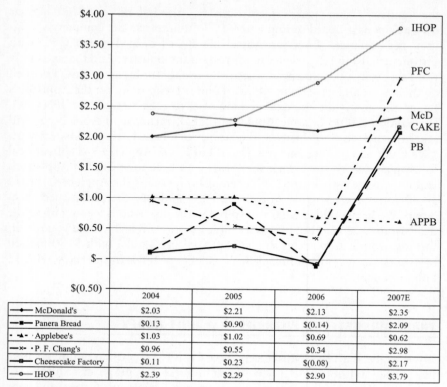

	2004	2005	2006	2007E
McDonald's	$2.03	$2.21	$2.13	$2.35
Panera Bread	$0.13	$0.90	$(0.14)	$2.09
Applebee's	$1.03	$1.02	$0.69	$0.62
P. F. Chang's	$0.96	$0.55	$0.34	$2.98
Cheesecake Factory	$0.11	$0.23	$(0.08)	$2.17
IHOP	$2.39	$2.29	$2.90	$3.79

EXHIBIT 7.16 Three Musketeers without New Unit Capex

Any ratio that says McDonald's, Applebee's, Panera Bread, and IHOP are more or less similar in regard to financial performance in the three-year period 2004 to 2006 is misleading. We have seen in the previous graphs that there are significant differences among these six companies in the generation (or lack thereof) of Free Cash Flow. The problem is that both of the components of ROE are full of accounting estimates. Do not blame the accountants for this problem. Financial analysts sometimes misuse accounting data in an attempt to simplify finance.

In addition, some public companies abuse their investors by bragging about *unit* investment returns when (1) the unit return numbers are undoubtedly influenced by accounting assumptions that are partially under management's control and (2) investor return is not determined by *unit* return but by *total* return: by changes in the company's Free Cash Flow and in its deployment. For example, P. F. Chang's 2006 Annual Report says they "... seek an average unit-level return on invested capital of 30 percent

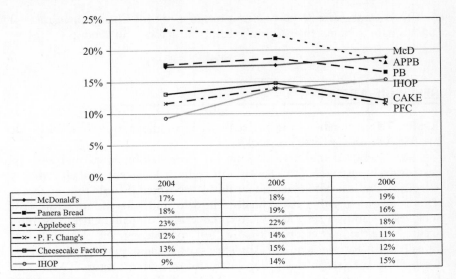

	2004	2005	2006
—♦— McDonald's	17%	18%	19%
—■— Panera Bread	18%	19%	16%
- ▲- · Applebee's	23%	22%	18%
—×- · P. F. Chang's	12%	14%	11%
—□— Cheesecake Factory	13%	15%	12%
—○— IHOP	9%	14%	15%

EXHIBIT 7.17 Return on Equity

and plan to continue to opening (sic) new restaurants to the extent that we continue to achieve our required rate of return."[4] Cheesecake Factory takes a similar approach. In a presentation to investors, Cheesecake management indicates a Grand Lux Café has a fully capitalized return target of 25 percent.[5] We agree 30 percent and 25 percent are pretty good returns. But how do we square 30 percent and 25 percent returns with Chang's and Cheesecake's anemic Free Cash Flows and their investor returns?

One of the major obstacles to understanding financial performance and investor return is a simple fact: Different people use the same words to mean different things. For example, McDonald's *Return* in the company's Return on Incremental Invested Capital applies to the entire company. That makes sense, because when investors buy shares of McDonald's stock, they are buying shares in the entire company. But our examples of Chang's and Cheesecake's uses of *return* refer to the return generated by *one new restaurant*. When we buy stock in Chang's or Cheesecake, are we buying stock in one new restaurant? Of course not. What do we care about more: the performance of one restaurant or the *entire* company's performance? Each new Chang's restaurant may well generate a 30 percent return, but Chang's high unit-growth strategy means Chang's investors will not likely see any of that 30 percent return for a long time to come. Because Chang's is taking every dollar of that 30 percent unit return and using it to build new restaurants. The 30 percent unit return is not for Chang's investors—it is for Chang's management, employees, contractors, and vendors.

SELL-SIDE ANALYSTS

Exhibit 7.18 summarizes the buy-sell-hold recommendations of the sell-side analysts who cover these six stocks.

These sell-side analysts spend most of their waking hours analyzing the restaurant industry. We can never hope to have 1 percent of their industry expertise. But is it not amazing that IHOP is covered by only four analysts? This is a company that reinvented itself, delivered outstanding returns for its investors and yet only four analysts cover the company. Cheesecake and Chang's are the only chains with any "Sell" or "Strong Sell" recommendations (except for the acquired Applebee's). Are there, perhaps, a few Free Cash Flow analysts in this group interested in investor return? Why does Cheesecake have more coverage than McDonald's and more "Strong Buy" ratings than all of the other companies? The Street worships Revenue and EPS growth. Restaurant analysts even express their concerns about these fast-growing chains reaching market saturation when, in fact, a significant *decline* in their unit growth would *increase* investor return. Not all analysts miss the boat, of course. Many sell-side analysts do an outstanding job. Still, as a group, sell-side analysts are compulsively positive about the companies they cover. A recent study reported that "... [S]ell-side analysts gave neutral-to-positive ratings 95.4 percent of the time."[6]

EXHIBIT 7.18 Analyst Recommendations

	Strong Buy	Buy	Hold	Sell	Strong Sell	Total
McDonald's	5	9	3	0	0	17
Panera Bread	5	1	11	0	0	17
Applebee's	2	0	16	1	1	20
P. F. Chang's	4	3	12	2	0	21
Cheesecake Factory	8	7	6	1	1	23
IHOP	1	2	1	0	0	4
Total	25	22	49	4	2	102

Note: As of July 2007.
Source: Yahoo!Finance.

EXHIBIT 7.19 Total Returns

	2004	2005	2006	2007
McDonald's	31.5	7.3	34.6	36.4
Panera Bread	2.0	62.9	−14.9	−35.9
Applebee's	1.1	−13.8	10.2	3.3*
P. F. Chang's	10.8	−11.9	−22.7	−40.5
Cheesecake Factory	10.6	15.2	−34.2	−3.6
IHOP	11.8	14.6	14.6	−29.4
Industry	36.8	7.5	24.8	9.9
S&P 500	9.0	3.0	13.6	3.5

Note: *Through 11/29/07.
Source: © Morningstar.[7]

TOTAL RETURNS

In this chapter we have compared the Free Cash Flow and EPS numbers and other metrics of the six companies. How well did these companies' investors do in the 2004–2007 period? Exhibit 7.19 shows the total returns (stock price plus dividends) of the six firms. We prefer to look at total return *numbers* rather than stock price *graphs* because stock graphs do not include dividends, if any, as do the Morningstar numbers in Exhibit 7.19. In addition, stock graphs provide fertile ground for counterproductive and time-wasting interpretations of historical price fluctuations.

These returns are more or less what a Free Cash Flow investor would expect. McDonald's has done very well for its investors in this period. The same cannot be said about Panera, Applebee's, Chang's and Cheesecake. The 2007 IHOP return reflects the predictable reaction of its Free Cash Flow investors to an eight-year payout of $1 billion of acquisition debt.

TAKE YOUR PICK

How does the Free Cash Flow Worksheet compare to the two equity models favored by the Street: EPS/PE and DCF? Exhibit 7.20 compares the three approaches by answering nine questions.

1. If EPS and PE are used to assess stocks, the investor is accepting all of the accounting estimates embedded in the EPS number. The only cash number in the entire analysis is the stock price. Some DCF models get

FREE CASH FLOW

EXHIBIT 7.20 Comparing Three Approaches

	EPS/PE	DCF	FCS/IR
1. Excludes accounting estimates?	No	No/Yes	Yes
2. Includes Δ Working Capital?	No	Yes	Yes
3. Includes Capex?	No	Yes	Yes
4. Includes Dividends?	No	No	Yes
5. Includes Δ Debt?	No	No	Yes
6. Captures investor return?	No	No	TBD
7. Usable by most investors?	Yes	No	Yes
8. Data-friendly?	Yes	Yes	No
9. Universal?	Yes	Yes	No

a *No* answer in Exhibit 7.20 because they use Operating Income or similar metric as the model's starting point. If so, the model is mixing apples and oranges by discounting accounting estimates. Some DCF models use Net CFO (Cash from Operations in the GAAP Cash Flow) so these models get a *Yes*. The Free Cash Flow per share/Investor Return model ("FCS/IR") depends on publicly disclosed financial statements. As we pointed out earlier, eliminating all of the charges and credits in the GAAP Cash Flow reduces but does not eliminate all accounting estimates. Still, we think a *Yes* is appropriate for FCS/IR.

2. This is a straightforward comparison although Working Capital, and particularly Δ Working Capital, are not always straightforward subjects.

3. DCF models and FCS/IR break out Capex.

4. FCS/IR is the only approach that includes dividend yield in a total return estimate. A typical Street research report provides a price target, and includes the dividend yield somewhere on the first page. But the price increase estimate and the dividend yield estimate are normally not combined into a total return number. Of course, such a combined number would still represent only a portion of our FCS/IR estimate. Perhaps we are asking too much?

5. The DCF model ignores a company's future debt levels. The DCF analysis subtracts *existing* total debt from the sum of the projected discounted cash flows and the terminal value. But where does that get us? Existing total debt is only the starting point of our FCS/IR debt analysis. The Δ Debt section of the Free Cash Flow Worksheet calculates an estimate of the change in debt because it is the *change* in a company's total debt that affects investor return going forward.

6. The EPS/PE scheme doesn't even address investor return, so there's no point in elaborating on the *No* answer for EPS/PE to the *capture* question. The DCF model produces an estimate of a stock's intrinsic or current share value. The current share value number is either higher, lower, or the same as the current market price. If the current share value estimate is sufficiently higher than the current market price, the stock may be recommended as a *buy* under the assumption that at some point in the future the market price will rise to the estimated share value. But the DCF valuation analysis addresses only current share value—it does not explicitly incorporate *future* dividend yield and *future* debt levels. Only the FCS/IR model captures (a) future changes in Free Cash Flow per share and (b) future dividends and (c) future changes in total debt and (d) incorporates a, b, and c into one investor return number that can be compared to the risks and returns of alternative investments. Yes, the FCS/IR model starts with the current market price and will be criticized for doing so. DCF modelers might say, "If the current market price overstates 'true' share value (as defined by the DCF model), you might buy a pig in a poke." No model is pig-proof, but if our analysis of a company suggests that (a), (b), and (c) will improve and if the company's results confirm our assumptions and analysis, the stock price should eventually benefit, absent material deterioration in the financial markets. We might well be wrong, of course, but at least we will be able to reassess our assumptions and hopefully do better the next time. In any event, the fact is the Free Cash Flow Worksheet is a new and unproven work-in-progress. That is why we put "TBD" for "to be determined" in the FCS/IR column. The Free Cash Flow Worksheet needs to be tested and improved by a large number of investors. Investors should only use the Free Cash Flow Worksheet as one element in a complete equity analysis.

7. If we reply *No* for the EPS/PE scheme, we must also reply *No* for the FCS/IR approach because all of the historical company data used in the FCS/IR analysis are taken from the GAAP financial statements. Since we do not want to give FCS/IR too many *No*'s, we will allow EPS/PE one *Yes*. Just as FCS/IR is not perfect, so EPS/PE is not perfectly imperfect. The DCF model requires the investor to do annual cash flow projections and decide on a cost of capital for the company being analyzed. The cost of capital is used to discount the projected cash flows and to compute the terminal, or residual value of the company. We have seen a number of valiant attempts to offer investors simplified versions of the DCF model. We have seen none succeed.

8. By *data-friendly,* we mean how easy is it for the investor to obtain public company data and use the data in a model? Since EPS/PE is

the dominant analytic, EPS investors have access to many free, for-fee, and custom data delivery options. Before manipulating or downloading data, EPS investors can review a boatload of historical data on any public company. The FCS/IR investor has access to the same data but must manually transfer data into the Free Cash Flow Worksheet. There is no public database of historical Operating Cash Flow Margins or deployments.

9. EPS/PE and DCF are universally acknowledged as the leading equity analytics. Each has a long history of application and usage. In the face of a million data points, convention provides comfort and security. Unsatisfactory results can be attributed to flawed application or incomplete due diligence. FCS/IR is new and unproven.

Each investor can critically evaluate the nine questions and answers. Are the questions skewed to favor FCS/IR over the also-rans? If so, what other questions should be asked? Are the answers on point? If not, why not? Does this discussion stimulate fresh thinking about equity analysis? In any event, prudent investors use more than one equity model. Those who decide to use the Free Cash Flow Worksheet should also use EPS/PE or DCF or some other model and take advantage of the benefits and insights of each approach.

In Chapter 8, we will "drill down" (as they say on the Street) into the CEO's annual letter to shareholders, the quarterly conference call, and the proxy and ask the question: What motivates the CEO?

CHAPTER 8

The CEO and Investor Return

In this chapter we assess how closely the CEO's priorities and objectives are aligned with investor return. Even if we employ the best financial metrics available, we will not obtain optimal returns unless we include in our company analysis a detailed assessment of the CEO. We start with the CEO's letter to shareholders in the annual report. Then we discuss the quarterly conference call and then the CEO's compensation package. We focus here on the letter, the call, and the comp package from *a Free Cash Flow perspective* because the CEO's impact on our return is critical and because we are unaware of other sources providing this perspective. To be sure, our focus here is a narrow one. There are many other due diligence issues that must be investigated by the equity analyst before making an investment decision.

THE CEO'S LETTER TO SHAREHOLDERS

In looking at the six CEO letters in the restaurant firms' 2006 annual reports, we address five questions:

1. Where do shareholders stand in the CEO's priorities, and is that reflected in the company's financial results and strategy?
2. Does the CEO define investor return, and is that definition consistent with our views?
3. Is the CEO's letter a complete accounting of the CEO's major decisions regarding investor return?
4. Does the CEO refer to any future activities that are likely to enhance or reduce investor returns?
5. Do the CEO's letter and the rest of the Annual Report suggest that management is aligned with investors?

McDonald's

1. *Where do shareholders stand in the CEO's priorities, and is that reflected in the company's financial results and strategy?*

Here is the first sentence of CEO Jim Skinner's letter to shareholders: "The first priority of all publicly held companies is to create long-term, profitable growth for shareholders."[1] Many CEO letters never specify the CEO's first priority. And when they do, it's often maximum sales or market leadership or happy customers. Of course the Free Cash Flow investor wants to confirm a declaration of "first priority" is likely to be backed up by the company's financial results and investor returns. The company's results—as reflected in Chapter 7's graphs and Total Returns Exhibit 7.19—support the CEO's statement.

2. *Does the CEO define investor return, and is that definition consistent with our views?*

The CEO's letter lists dividends, buybacks, and stock price as the sources of investor return. This is essentially consistent with our concept of investor return. His letter emphasizes "cash return to shareholders" and says McDonald's in 2006 returned $4.9 billion in cash to shareholders in the form of dividends and buybacks.[2] The company's 2006 GAAP Statement of Cash Flows indicates the amount was only $4.2 billion. The source of the $700 million difference is obscured by GAAP accounting fog.

3. *Is the CEO's letter a complete accounting of the CEO's major decisions regarding investor return?*

The CEO's letter highlighted the dividends and buybacks but unfortunately did not mention the stock options exercised. In 2006, McDonald's received $976 million in proceeds from employees who exercised stock options. Those new shares wiped out roughly a third of the buybacks' gain for shareholders. Going forward, McDonald's says it's reducing the use of options and replacing them with other nondilutive benefits. Still, management should not take full credit for buybacks if the exercise of stock options materially dilutes the impact of buybacks on investor return.

4. *Does the CEO indicate any future activities that can enhance or reduce investor returns?*

The CEO letter does not address specific plans, but the text of the Annual Report makes several important points: (1) McDonald's will allocate at least $5 billion to dividends and share repurchases in 2007–2008; (2) equity-tied compensation will decline; (3) low-return company and franchise units will be converted to a franchise arrangement that requires no McDonald's capital, and (4) company operations are evaluated using a ROIC model that imposes capital utilization discipline on the organization (the ROIC model is a GAAP-based model, but nobody's perfect).[3]

5. *Do the CEO's letter and the rest of the Annual Report suggest that management is aligned with investors?*

Most of the comments offered here, plus the company's financial results through 2006, suggest this CEO has investor interests at the top of his priority list. As CEO, he must strike a balance among conflicting objectives and groups. It is difficult to imagine a better job of changing course and executing the first restructuring program.

Panera Bread

1. *Where do shareholders stand in the CEO's priorities, and is that reflected in the company's financial results and strategy?*

Panera's CEO mentions shareholders twice in his 2007 letter to shareholders. In the final paragraph, he offers shareholders the obligatory "...thank you for believing in and supporting our vision...."[3] The second mention is in the form of a direct, urgent appeal by the CEO to shareholders: "If you haven't already, we encourage you to try Crispani."[4] Crispani is Panera's new pizza, served after 4 P.M.

2. *Does the CEO define investor return, and is that definition consistent with our views?*

This is really stretching it, but here is the second sentence of the letter: "Earnings per share (EPS) came in at $1.84, placing us once again among the highest-growth companies in our industry."[5]

3. *Is the CEO's letter a complete accounting of the CEO's major decisions regarding investor return?*

Yes.

4. *Does the CEO indicate any future activities that can enhance or reduce investor returns?*

Investors who buy a boatload of Crispani will find their reward.

5. *Do the CEO's letter and the rest of the Annual Report suggest that management is aligned with investors?*

The CEO's "Dear Shareholder" letter says the CEO's priorities are customers, employees, and members of his Board. It is not clear where investors fit in.

Applebee's

1. *Where do shareholders stand in the CEO's priorities, and is that reflected in the company's financial results and strategy?*

This is a tough one. At the time of the annual report, David L. Goebel had been CEO for roughly six months. He acknowledges in the letter that the company is for sale. He does say many of the things Free Cash Flow investors like to hear: "We remain committed to having a highly disciplined approach to capital allocation and to focusing on relevant long-term strategies to drive shareholder value, including increasing Free Cash Flow generation through a significant reduction in capital expenditures and new unit development in 2007."[5]

2. *Does the CEO define investor return, and is that definition consistent with our views?*

The CEO obliquely acknowledges the importance of his shareholders' "total return" by the naming of the Applebee's Leadership Institute after the previous CEO. During his predecessor's reign, the CEO says, ". . . Applebee's total return to shareholders exceeded 300 percent, a compound annual growth rate of more than 17 percent."[6]

3. *Is the CEO's letter a complete accounting of the CEO's major decisions regarding investor return?*

In 2006, Applebee's exercised stock options were about 45% of the buybacks. The CEO took credit for the buybacks but did not mention the option exercises.

4. *Does the CEO indicate any future activities that can enhance or reduce investor return?*

Our comments in Chapter 7 regarding the IHOP/Applebee deal describe the events that followed the CEO's March 2006 letter.

5. *Do the CEO's letter and the rest of the Annual Report suggest that management is aligned with investors?*

Again, Mr. Goebel had been CEO for only six months when he signed the letter. He is no longer with Applebee's.

P. F. Chang's Bistro

1. *Where do shareholders stand in the CEO's priorities, and is that reflected in the company's financial results and strategy?*

The first sentence of the letter, addressed to "Fellow Stockholders," is: "The primary mission of our company is to continue to be the best operator of Asian restaurants as viewed by our guests and our employees."[7]

2. *Does the CEO define investor return, and is that definition consistent with our views?*

The CEO says his restaurants ". . . provide top of class returns to our stockholders."[8] According to Morningstar, P. F. Chang's Total Returns in 2005 and 2006 were −11.9 percent and −22.7 percent respectively, as compared to Industry Total Returns of 7.5 percent and 24.8 percent, respectively.[9] It is unclear how the CEO defines *class* and *returns*.

3. *Is the CEO's letter a complete accounting of the CEO's major decisions regarding investor return?*

   Yes.

4. *Does the CEO indicate any future activities that can enhance or reduce investor returns?*

   The CEO affirms: "...[W]e learned some valuable lessons around self-cannibalization . . ." and he assures us he ". . . [W]ill apply the lessons learned from these experiences. . . ." as they grow.[10]

5. *Do the CEO's letter and the rest of the Annual Report suggest that management is aligned with investors?*

   It is hard to find evidence of alignment.

Cheesecake Factory

1. *Where do shareholders stand in the CEO's priorities, and is that reflected in the company's financial results and strategy?*

   There's not much to go on here.

2. *Does the CEO define investor return, and is that definition consistent with our views?*

   Ditto.

3. *Is the CEO's letter a complete accounting of the CEO's major decisions regarding investor return?*

   Yes.

4. *Does the CEO indicate any future activities that can enhance or reduce investor returns?*

   The CEO says the Grand Lux Cafe should be able to grow from eight to 150 units.[11]

5. *Do the CEO's letter and the rest of the Annual Report suggest that management is aligned with investors?*

   There does not appear to be much evidence of material alignment. If the company going forward manages to Free Cash Flow and does as good a job with that as it has with restaurant management, good things should happen to Cheesecake investors.

IHOP

1. *Where do shareholders stand in the CEO's priorities, and is that reflected in the company's financial results and strategy?*

   The CEO's letter emphasizes the importance of maximum cash flow and minimum Capex, as well as dividends and buybacks, as key components of the company's strategy.

2. *Does the CEO define investor return, and is that definition consistent with our views?*

The CEO says, "Our total shareholder return is one of the best in the industry and now exceeds 150 percent, reflecting our stock price performance and dividend payments from the beginning of 2003 through February 2007."[12]

3. *Is the CEO's letter a complete accounting of the CEO's major decisions regarding investor return?*

IHOP's stock option exercises were roughly 10 percent of buybacks. The option exercises are not mentioned in the letter, but at 10 percent that is not a big issue. The CEO takes credit, however, for borrowing to do buybacks, thereby purportedly ". . . enhancing shareholder value and driving earnings per share growth in 2007."[13] A significant increase in debt can reduce share value unless the debt proceeds generate incremental Free Cash Flow and the debt is reduced in a reasonable timeframe.

4. *Does the CEO indicate any future activities that can enhance or reduce investor returns?*

No IHOP investor could possibly have been blindsided by the acquisition of Applebee's after reading the CEO's letter. Ms. Stewart states: ". . . [W]e will continue to seek out and evaluate acquisition opportunities in 2007."[14] Our take on IHOP's acquisition of Applebee's is in Chapter 7.

5. *Do the CEO's letter and the rest of the Annual Report suggest that management is aligned with investors?*

Our answer is both "Yes" and "No." Yes, because the CEO's strategy up to the time of the letter was brilliantly conceived and executed. Everything in the letter is exceptional—except for the comments about wanting to do an acquisition and funding buybacks with debt.

Here again are the Total Returns of the six companies (see Exhibit 8.1).

The investor must assess the CEO's priorities and the CEO's understanding of investor return. If the annual letter says nothing substantive about these two subjects, that raises a question. The answer may well be to move on to the next stock on the list. But what if the CEO hits almost all of our high notes—like in Applebee's letter? Words are free. The numbers come first. Still, the CEO is one of the most important factors in our investment decision. If a CEO specifically addresses our top concerns as the CEO of McDonald's did in the annual letter, that's a plus but only because this CEO's words are supported by sound financial strategy and results. The McDonald's CEO understands the CEO's three jobs:

EXHIBIT 8.1 Total Returns

	2004	2005	2006	2007
McDonald's	31.5	7.3	34.6	36.4
Panera Bread	2.0	62.9	−14.9	−35.9
Applebee's	1.1	−13.8	10.2	3.3*
P. F. Chang's	10.8	−11.9	−22.7	−40.5
Cheesecake Factory	10.6	15.2	−34.2	−3.6
IHOP	11.8	14.6	14.6	−29.4
Industry	36.8	7.5	24.8	9.9
S&P 500	9.0	3.0	13.6	3.5

*Through 11/29/07.
Source: ©Morningstar.[7]

The CEO's Three Jobs
- Chief Revenue Officer
- Chief Margin Officer
- Chief Capital Officer

Because we are focused on financial performance, we confine our *Jobs* to those of a financial nature. Chief People Officer and Chief Ethics Officer are equally important responsibilities.

THE QUARTERLY EARNINGS CONFERENCE CALL

Our next information source is the quarterly earnings conference call. Four times a year the CEO and CFO address investors and analysts and take their questions. What do we look for in a call? We're looking for the same things we looked for in the CEO letter. Do the CEO and CFO explicitly address investor return issues or do they simply brag about increased Revenues and EPS? The quarterly call is critical to investors because it is when analysts and institutional investors ask management about the prospects for the next quarter and next year. They ask about future Revenues, margins, Capex, and tax rates so they can build their EPS or DCF models. Not coincidentally, these are the same things we want to quantify so we can use the Free Cash Flow Worksheet.

The quarterly call should be a public dialogue on the fundamental drivers of the company's return potential. However, the scope of the call is restricted if the company has not filed the 10-Q or K in advance of the call. That's because the press release always appears before the call but does not include the Notes to the Statements that are in the Q's and K. Consequently, the Q&A portion of the call is not based on complete financial statements unless the Q or K is available *before* the call. In any event, the CEO's script begins the call and is followed by the CFO's script. Listen to how closely aligned the CEO and CFO are in regard to the company's priorities and prospects. Again, as return investors, we are concerned about the prospects for whatever affects Free Cash Flow and its deployment. Anything about existing and future Capex projects is especially important because with some companies we'll get more Capex information in the quarterly call than any printed source. Management's attitude toward acquisitions can also surface in a more revealing manner during the call than in print. Beware the CEO whose tone of voice and comments convey a determination to do an acquisition.

The meat of most calls is the Q&A. No one expects CEOs and CFOs to have all the answers at their fingertips. But they should have the answers to almost all the questions asked by analysts and investors. The author has prepared any number of Q&A question lists for many management teams. A list of potential questions about the contents of the press release and about issues not in the press release is compiled. Then the list is reviewed in a practice session with the CEO and CFO to make sure they are prepared. Listen to which analysts ask softball questions and which analysts ask return-related questions. When reading these analysts' research reports, keep these observations in mind. Also, grade the CEO on how well the questions are answered. It is not uncommon for CEOs to ignore some questions. They may not want to discuss a particular subject for competitive reasons. That's fine, as long as every subject of interest is not labeled "competitive." If that is the case, there are plenty of other public companies.

The Q&A is an opportunity to assess CEOs operating in an unrehearsed, script-less situation. Do they actually answer the question that was asked or do they skirt or ignore the question? Some CEOs are skilled at filibustering questions they cannot or will not answer, talking as fast and as long as they can so as to envelop the answer in so much verbal dust that people think the question was answered when it was not. Before investing in a company, listen to the most recent call and another call from a year or so ago. A one year time gap between calls should provide a pretty good perspective on the CEO. Many CEOs get carried away with their enthusiasm and optimism, especially on the conference call. Do they chronically issue overly optimistic predictions about future Revenues, market share, or new products? When they say they are going to do something by a certain time, do they do it in the specified time frame? We do not have total recall, so we, at best, only remember promises made in last quarter's call. Make a note of CEO promises in a worksheet and track how well they deliver on their promises. When they do not meet their promises, do they provide lame excuses, acknowledge shortcomings in execution or do they simply forget about the promises? Also, make sure there are no land mines in the 10-Q or 10-K Notes that were not revealed in the related press release or conference call. This happens more often than many investors realize. One last point: When looking at the press releases and listening to the calls over a period of a year or so, be on the lookout for major changes in a company's financial operations. Three examples would be the press releases by IHOP and McDonald's announcing their restructuring programs and the Cheesecake press release on their scaled back Capex program. These changes can sometimes be signs of meaningful investor opportunities ahead.

THE CEO'S INCENTIVE COMPENSATION

Before taking a position in a company's common stock, Free Cash Flow investors must know the components of the CEO's compensation package. If a CEO's compensation package is based primarily on increases in company EPS or increases in Revenues, we must question the the CEOs committment to investor return.

Go to the investor section of the company's web site or go to EDGAR at sec.gov/edgar/searchedgar/companysearch.html.

Type in the company's ticker and look for the latest 14A proxy filing. The proxy is issued before each Annual Meeting and provides information on issues to be addressed in the Annual Meeting as well as information on management compensation and Board committee activities. Our objective in this exercise is not to evaluate the company's overall compensation program as compared to their peers or the intricate details of the options program. Instead, we'll address only this question:

Is the CEO's annual compensation package based on one or more of the following:

- EPS or other GAAP metric(s)?
- Free Cash Flow per share or other cash flow metric(s)?
- Company stock price?
- Dividends?

If we are looking at a company the size of McDonald's, the proxy's executive compensation section is long and fairly complex. Fortunately, we are only looking at a small part of the compensation section. After looking at the comp sections of three or four companies, the investor can quickly go through most companies' comp sections.

EXHIBIT 8.2   CEO Incentive Compensation Matrix

| | Linkage Between CEO Compensation and: | | | |
	EPS or Other GAAP Metric	Free Cash Flow or Other Cash Flow Metric	Company Stock Price	Investor Total Return
McDonald's	Yes	No	Yes	Yes
Panera Bread	Yes	No	No	No
Applebee's	Yes	No	No	Yes
P. F. Chang's	Yes	No	No	No
Cheesecake Factory	No	No	No	No
IHOP	No	Yes	Yes	Yes

Note: Per 2007 Proxy filings.

We looked at the comp sections of the six companies to find out which financial performance metrics are incorporated in their incentive compensation packages. Exhibit 8.2 summarizes the linkage between CEO incentive compensation and the metrics at the top of each column. "Investor Total Return" in Exhibit 8.2 is stock price plus dividends.

It is interesting to note that *all but one* of these companies' proxies assert that executive compensation is designed *to align company performance with shareholder return.* Which of the six companies did *not* make that claim? We answer the question at the end of this section. We will go through the comp sections of each company to get a flavor of what you might find.

McDonald's

The McDonald's 2007 proxy states: "EPS was selected as an appropriate performance measure for our executives because they are in a position to control the strategic direction of the Company."[15] That is true, but it is also the case that GAAP's flexibility allows some of the executives to affect McDonald's' EPS. Having said that, McDonald's should be given credit for reducing its total options grants as a percentage of total shares outstanding over the last several years.

In addition to salary, perks, and annual cash bonus, the McDonald's CEO receives stock options, restricted stock units, and a three-year cash incentive plan. The cash incentive plan is based on the company's operating income, return on assets, and cumulative total shareholder return (stock price plus dividends) as compared to the S&P 500 Index. How much of the CEO's comp package is affected by total shareholder return? The proxy says the impact of the total shareholder return was 7.5 percent on the payout of the 2004–2006 cash incentive plan. The CEO's payout under this plan was $5.3 million. His total 2006 comp package was $12.7 million.[16] So it appears the CEO would survive even if the stock price fell. In any event, we urge investors not to ignore human nature. The fact that a portion of the CEO's compensation package is affected by the stock price and dividend rate is important because it directly aligns the CEO's interests with investors' intertests.

Also, McDonald's has adopted restricted stock units (RSUs). Priest and McClelland point out in *Free Cash Flow and Shareholder Yield* that ". . . RSUs represent a compensation-related incentive for companies to pay dividends that did not exist previously," because ". . . all shareholders receive the benefits of dividends, including management."[17] Would we be happier if the CEO's package were based on Free Cash Flow per share rather than operating income? Sure, because what if McDonald's changes their financial strategy or other factors come into play and their EPS and FCS materially diverge? What if they get a new CEO? A new CEO means we are essentially looking at a new stock.

We applaud McDonald's for including return on investment as an element of the long-term incentive plan. Yes, it is calculated with GAAP numbers, but at least the company incorporates capital utilization in executive compensation.

Panera Bread

Here is a quote from Panera Bread's 2007 proxy: ". . . [O]ur executive compensation program has been specifically designed to reinforce achievement of earnings based metrics, rewarding sustainable growth in earnings in order to increase the overall equity value of our Company."[18] We do not know how Panera defines "equity value."

Applebee's

Applebee's compensation package is true to form: inconsistent. At least the Applebee's Compensation Committee conceptually concedes the wisdom of excluding the buybacks' benefit in the calculation of EPS. Here is a quote from Applebee's proxy for the 2007 annual meeting:

> *In certain exceptional circumstances, the (Compensation) Commit-*
> *tee may determine to remove the effect of certain items from the*
> *earnings per share calculation. These could include the impact of*
> *significant stock repurchases, one-time non-cash accounting charges*
> *or stock-based compensation awards. In 2006, only stock-based*
> *compensation awards were excluded from the earnings per share*
> *performance metrics.*[19]

Applebee's did $38 million in buybacks in 2006 and $196 million in buybacks in 2005. According to their quote, the Board did not exclude the impact of the $38 million buyback on the 2006 bonus calculation of EPS. Question: Did the Applebee's Board of Directors exclude the benefit of the $196 million buybacks in the 2005 calculation of EPS for the executive comp packages? We do not know the answer to that question because Applebee's proxy for the 2006 meeting said nothing about the EPS calculation for the 2005 executive comp packages. The members of the Applebee's Compensation Committee undoubtedly thought it so obvious the impact of buybacks would be excluded in the calculation of bonuses that they didn't want to insult shareholders by mentioning it. We saw no mention of a buyback exclusion from the EPS calculation in the other five companies' proxies.

P. F. Chang's Bistro

Someone at P. F. Chang's noticed that their executive officers were paid below the median of their industry peer group. The Compensation Committee of the Board rode to the rescue. This is a quote from Chang's proxy:

> . . . *[T]he Committee set targeted compensation for the executive*
> *officers at the 75th percentile of compensation paid to similarly*
> *situated executives of the companies comprising the peer group.*
> *Variations to this objective may occur as dictated by the experience*
> *level of the individual and market factors. These objectives recognize*
> *the Committee's expectation that, over the long term, the Company*
> *will continue to generate stockholder returns in excess of the average*
> *of its peer group.*[20]

Here's another quote from Chang's 2007 proxy:

> *No payments were made to the executive officers under the Bonus Plan for 2006 due to the fact that the Company did not achieve as of the end of the Company's fiscal year 2006 the minimum target level of Restaurant Cash Operating Income required to trigger a distribution to the executive officers.*
>
> *The Committee approved the fiscal year 2007 Bonus Plan at its February 5, 2007 meeting. Payouts, if any, under the 2007 Bonus Plan will be based on the achievement by the Company of targeted earnings per share levels during fiscal year 2007. The Company believes that the shift to earnings per share as the basis for determining payouts under the 2007 Bonus Plan more closely aligns the compensation of the participants under the Bonus Plan with delivery of increased value to stockholders, than the use of Restaurant Cash Operating Income.[21]*

Chang's is actually going *backward* as far as share value is concerned—from some kind of *cash* metric to EPS—so that its executives can get their *cash* bonuses. The directors say the shift was made in the interests of "increased value to shareholders." It is curious that the buy-side has recently been demanding more detailed information on executive compensation, yet some of them do not seem to use the information already in the proxy.

Cheesecake Factory

In 2004 the Board of Directors established a scheduled annual increase in the CEO's salary for the period 2004–2008. At the same time they granted the CEO in each of these years at least 100,000 shares of stock. The CEO is also eligible for cash bonuses based on "financial results" and other factors. True, the CEO founded the company and Cheesecake is what it is because of him. And if this were a private company, the CEO would not know what to do with all the compensation he could take out. But the Cheesecake Factory is not a private company. CEO compensation should be affected at least in part by investor return and those metrics that drive investor return. Why then did the Board fix the CEO's salary increases and option grants? The Cheesecake 2007 proxy says:

> *The Compensation Committee concluded that Mr. Overton's compensation, including stock option grants, significantly benefit us and*

*our stockholders by securing Mr. Overton's services for the future
and thereby motivating him to continue his focus on our long-term
strategic growth and profitability.*[22]

Apparently the Cheesecake Board feared the CEO might suddenly abandon the company he conceived and built. What other restaurant company
did the Board think would steal their CEO? Wendy's? Weinerschnitzel?

IHOP

There are no long-winded platitudes about "aligning management and shareholders interests" in the IHOP proxy. There is no need for empty claims of
alignment because IHOP's compensation program and company performance are aligned. Here's how the CEO's bonus is determined:

> *Payouts are earned for achieving specified business objectives for
> total shareholder return relative to an index of peer companies and
> aggregate net cash flow from operations, over a three-year period
> beginning January 1, 2004 and ending December 31, 2006 (the
> "Performance Period"). In order to reach the minimum threshold
> for payouts, the Company's relative total shareholder return for
> the Performance Period must be at or above the 35th percentile, as
> compared to the peer index, or the Company's cumulative aggregate
> net cash flow from operations for the Performance Period must be
> equal to or greater than $140,000,000. In order to reach the max-
> imum payout, the Company's relative total shareholder return for
> the performance period must be at or above the 65th percentile, as
> compared to the peer index, and the Company's cumulative aggre-
> gate net cash flow from operations for the three-year period must
> be equal to or greater than $190,000,000.*[23]

Make sure to note that the *or* following the *35th percentile* changed to
an *and* following the *65th percentile*.

This is alignment. It renders the *claims* of alignment, pronounced in
many of the proxies filed with and accepted by the SEC, egregiously disin-
genuous. Still, alignment is a necessary but not sufficient element in an
investment decision.

Let's leave IHOP and conclude the CEO compensation section with a
general point about CEO bonus computations. In Chapter 4, we noted that
management can manipulate Working Capital accounts to reduce Working
Capital and thereby increase Free Cash Flow. For example, Days Payables
can be sharply increased to generate additional cash in a quarter by reducing

cash payments to vendors. Some commentators argue that Free Cash Flow should therefore not be used as an executive bonus target because Working Capital and Capex can be easily manipulated by management without being subject to GAAP. We do not agree. The board of directors can structure the compensation calculations so that Working Capital and other accounts cannot be used by management to inflate Free Cash Flow per share. For example, the board can retroactively adjust actual Free Cash Flow per share to the extent, say, Days' Payables moved above a restricted limit.

We have explored Free Cash Flow and deployment. How do we go about using these concepts to find great stocks? Chapter 9 offers suggestions on using Free Cash Flow in stock screening and analysis.

CHAPTER 9

Finding Great Stocks

It should come as no surprise that the Free Cash Flow investor finds great stocks by incorporating the Free Cash Flow Worksheet into the investor's existing equity analysis discipline. Each investor who decides to adopt some or all of the Free Cash Flow/deployment/investor return model will decide how to integrate this approach into the investor's existing analytical and due diligence process. The Nine Steps are only our suggestions as to how to get started in adapting our model to your existing routines.

THE NINE STEPS

Step 1: Conduct a Knowledge-Based Search for Candidates and Only Then Use Screeners

The easiest way to become familiar with the Free Cash Flow Worksheet is to use it first on current portfolio holdings. These are the companies with which the investor is most familiar. The historical statements and other company data are at hand. Inputting a company's historical numbers into Free Cash Flow Worksheet should be a straightforward exercise. A one-year projection should not require much incremental research, although those elements in the Free Cash Flow Worksheet that are not currently part of the investor's analysis may need some attention. The Free Cash Flow Worksheet may well shed new light on some of your current holdings. After comparing the different stocks with the Worksheet, the investor may look differently on some stocks in the portfolio.

An alternative is to choose several industries with which the investor is most familiar. An industry-focused stock search offers several advantages over general market screening. The investor who uses the Worksheet to compare companies in the same industry and applies industry knowledge to the comparisons develops a clearer appreciation of the opportunities and

145

risks underlying the numbers. The investor can learn facts and insights while working on one company and apply them to other companies in the same industry. This compound effect gives the investor an advantage over EPS generalists whose industry comparisons are based on misleading metrics and a shallow financial understanding of future industry trends. Several banking assignments as an industry specialist in airlines, aerospace companies, and insurance provided the author with extensive evidence of the benefits of industry focus. It is difficult to assess a CEO's analysis of current and future industry trends without comparing the CEO's comments to those of other CEO's in the same industry.

The following comments apply to professional investors and individual investors who use free or for-fee screeners. The Free Cash Flow investor must exercise caution in using stock screeners. First, be aware that stock screeners appear and disappear on a regular basis. Screeners that do not disappear are subject to major upgrades that sometimes are really unwelcome downgrades. Try to use two screeners so that a backup is always available in the event the preferred screener is removed from the market. There is another benefit to using two screeners. The Free Cash Flow investor's preferred screener may not be able to handle a desired screen. This is a common problem because free and low-fee screeners are aimed at EPS investors, not Free Cash Flow investors. By using two screeners, the investor can sometimes complete the desired screen. For example, an investor wants to find all companies with: (1) market cap over $100 million and (2) Revenue growth in last three years over 15 percent and (3) the percentile rank of the company's annual return versus the industry return and (4) Capex as a percentage of Revenues under 10 percent. Assume the preferred screener can handle (1), (2), and (3), but not (4). If the back-up screener can handle (4), then the investor can run both screens and merge the results of the two screeners. The companies that appear in the results of both screens satisfy all four requirements.

Here are several questions to address when choosing and using stock screeners:

1. How many stocks are covered by the screener? Some screeners cover a lot more companies than other screeners.
2. Are screen results downloadable into Excel? If not, it will take time to transfer the results into Excel should you want to sort companies in Excel. It will also be harder to merge results of different screeners to form a candidate list.
3. How does the screener define *each term* that you want to screen for? This is the most problematic aspect of using free or for-fee screeners. Different screeners use different definitions for the same terms. More often than not, definitions of Free Cash Flow and related metrics are

flawed. For example, Free Cash Flow is defined in the following ways by four different screeners:

- Cash provided by operating activities minus Capex
- Cash provided by operating activities minus Capex minus dividends
- Cash receipts minus cash payments over a given period of time; or equivalently, net profit plus amounts charged off for depreciation, depletion, and amortization
- Net income + depreciation + amortization $+/-\Delta$WC $-$ (Capex + dividends)

The first definition is the only one that yields the same number as our definition of Free Cash Flow. The other definitions are either problematic or unclear. When definitions are unclear, it's best to run a screen and then compare the screen's variable results for several companies to the investor's own calculations using the companies' financial statements.

Some investors will gravitate toward Free Cash Flow Yield (or a variant thereof) as a primary screen. By looking only at stocks in the top quartile or top half of Free Cash Flow Yields, these investors may think they are building a margin of safety into the screen. But it is equally plausible that some of the best return candidates can be found in the bottom quartile of Free Cash Flow Yields. Some of these are companies that may have recently transitioned from negative to positive Free Cash Flow and may have good prospects for continued growth in Free Cash Flow. Dividend yield is a popular screen. Those investors still heavily focused on dividend yield, as opposed to total return, should reread the dividend section in Chapter 5 before using dividend yield as a primary screen.

Step 2: Take a Quick Look

After finding stock candidates from industry searches, screens, *Barron's*, the *Wall Street Journal*, and other sources, take a quick look at each candidate before inputting its historical financials into the Free Cash Flow Worksheet. The quick look can be done in many free or for-fee financial web sites. Eyeball the last two or three years of Revenue growth, Cash provided by operating activities, Δ Working Capital, Capex, acquisitions, buybacks or shares issued, and debt trends. A high percentage of companies will be eliminated by a quick visual tour of basic financial data. *Eliminate* companies that have been generating negative Free Cash Flow unless a rough trend line suggests the company may soon reach positive Free Cash Flow. The last time we screened for positive Free Cash Flow only, roughly 3,600 companies survived the screen. That is a pretty big haystack in which to begin a stock search. Stay away from companies that are frequent acquirers unless you are knowledgeable about the industry. Not coincidentally, many serial acquirers are chronic generators of negative Free Cash Flow. Investors should minimize exposure to companies with new CEOs. A new CEO makes it more difficult than usual to project Free Cash Flow/deployment.

Step 3: Input Historical Free Cash Flow Statements into the Free Cash Flow Worksheet

Until there is a publicly available database that offers investors access to public company financials in the Free Cash Flow/deployment/investor return format, investors must input historical data into the Free Cash Flow Worksheet. Some companies that passed the "Quick Look" will be disqualified when the historical Free Cash Flow Statement is completed. The investor may see disqualifying numbers in the Free Cash Flow Statement or in the Percentages, Per Share Data, Incremental Data, or Company's Reinvestment Return.

Step 4: Input Historical Cash Sources and Cash Deployments into the Worksheet

Look at how management has generated cash and deployed cash in recent years. The recent past is, for now, a fairly good indicator of the near-term future. An exception is a company the investor is considering primarily because of imminent changes in cash flow management likely to benefit investors. Proceed to Step 5 if the company appears to respect its investors.

Step 5: Project Free Cash Flow

This is the fun part! Some investors will employ a quick-and-dirty estimate here and, if the company passes, conduct due diligence to make a serious estimate. Others will conduct due diligence first and then make an estimate. It may be helpful to review the discussion in Chapters 4 and 5 about the components of the Free Cash Flow Statement and the four deployments. If the company's projected Free Cash Flow appears promising, proceed to Step 6.

Step 6: Project Cash Sources and Cash Deployments

Keep in mind that many companies do not (1) make acquisitions or (2) buyback or issue shares or (3) pay dividends or (4) have debt. Many firms do only one or two out of (1)–(4).That means the investor can sometimes quickly complete this Step. To be sure, many companies do three or four. Chances are the investor will encounter a mix of companies in this Step 6. If the total investor return in cell B145 looks promising, proceed to the Return Multiple.

Step 7: Use the Return Multiple

The Return Multiple may feel a bit awkward at first but give it a fair try. As we stated in Chapter 6, use of the Return Multiple does not eliminate the chances of unacceptable returns but it should enhance the investor's appreciation of the relationship between risk and opportunity. If the Return Multiple suggests the company's stock offers an acceptable return for the risk compared to alternative investments, complete the due diligence process. A small but critical part of the due diligence analysis is the CEO Exam.

Step 8: Conduct the CEO Exam

The results of the Free Cash Flow Worksheet exercise combined with the annual shareholders' letter, the proxy section on executive compensation, the company's yes-or-no answers in the CEO Comp Matrix, and the quarterly conference calls provide the investor with sufficient information to address a key question: Who is the CEO working for? Is the CEO working for the company's investors? Or is the CEO primarily working for the CEO, employees, vendors, and customers? Some CEOs work very hard for all of the company's constituencies yet understand that investors deserve priority treatment. Some CEOs appear to be clueless about financial matters, issuing platitudes about higher sales and higher earnings while they're running the company's share value and its investors' returns into the ground. Investors must show no mercy when a CEO fails the exam. Drop the company and move on to the next candidate. The investor's assessment of the CEO is no less important than the results of the Free Cash Flow Worksheet. Even if the company offers acceptable returns, there are countless other companies run by serious, responsible CEOs who understand and respect investor return as much as they understand their business and know how to generate sound financial results. This kind of CEO effectively executes her responsibilities as Chief Revenue Officer, Chief Margin Officer, and Chief Capital Officer. When such a CEO leaves a company in the investor's portfolio for another company, follow the CEO's progress at her next company and be ready to buy if it appears to be a good investment. Be sure, however, to consider the aforementioned risk of investing in a company with a new CEO. Having said that, a great CEO is a terrible thing for an investor to lose.

Step 9: Buy Sell Hold

The Free Cash Flow investor's buy/sell/hold decision is not three different decisions. It is the same decision made in the same, disciplined sequence regardless of the investor's share ownership status. The only question is: Does this stock offer the required return (as projected in the Free Cash Flow Worksheet) appropriate to the risk (as provided in the Return Multiple)? If after due diligence and analysis the investor decides the answer is "Yes," then the investor buys the stock if it is not in the portfolio (or puts the stock on a watch list if there are better candidates). If a "Yes" stock is already in the portfolio, the investor holds the stock until the next analysis. If the answer is "No," the investor does not add the stock to the portfolio. If a "No" stock is already in the portfolio, the investor sells the stock. Because the Free Cash Flow investor takes a comprehensive, economic and disciplined approach to equity investing, the Free Cash Flow investor is not vulnerable to the constant barrage of "when to buy" and "when to sell" nonsense that passes as Street wisdom. Our nine steps to great stocks are a suggested initial path. Each investor will eventually find a sequence that works best.

DIVERSIFICATION FOR INDIVIDUAL INVESTORS

People ask how many stocks they should have in their retirement portfolios. Rule Number 1 is: Ignore many of today's most popular investing books. So-called professional investors are advising their readers to invest all of their money in only a few stocks—say six or eight stocks—and to watch those stocks like a hawk. This is reckless, irresponsible baloney. Diversification is the single most important principle of sound investing. Of course, the investor must closely watch each portfolio stock. But there will always be surprises, and stop/loss orders will not always prevent losses because of gap openings or trading gaps during market hours. What's a gap? Let's say an investor has a stop/loss order with his broker at $45. The stock closed yesterday at $50 but it opens today at $25 because there was bad news after yesterday's closing. The stop/loss order is rendered irrelevant at today's market opening by the sudden avalanche of sell orders.

The investor should decide how much money he can afford to lose because one stock evaporates overnight. An affordable loss presumably is one that does not materially affect current or retirement lifestyle. Think about the tolerable magnitude of such a loss and then make that amount the maximum limit for any one stock in the portfolio. That maximum dollar limit for each stock roughly determines how many stocks should be in the portfolio. Total dollars in the equity portfolio divided by the maximum limit for each stock equals the minimum number of stocks. Here's an example using $25,000 as the Maximum Loss and $400,000 as the total equity portfolio investment.

$$\frac{\text{Equity Portfolio}}{\text{Maximum Loss}} = \frac{\$400,000}{\$25,000} = 16 \text{ Stocks} \qquad (9.1)$$

When a stock exceeds the Maximum Loss limit, the investor must sell the excess portion and reinvest it. The minimum stock calculation can be adjusted to reflect expected return between now and liquidation. The key point is to reject the current fad in portfolio construction. Concentrating retirement assets in a few "great" stocks is a terrible idea.

EQUITY MUTUAL FUNDS

Let's say the investor in our Maximum Loss example can't find 16 stocks. He can only find nine stocks that meet his requirements for return, risk, and diversification. In that case, the investor has the option of using equity mutual funds for the remaining $175,000 to fill out the equity portfolio. As is the case with individual stocks, mutual fund returns for the last year or multiple years don't tell us what the returns will be next year. How does the individual investor go about selecting good actively managed mutual funds rather than chase historical fund returns? First, the investor should develop a list of mutual fund candidates that meet diversification goals. Then find each mutual fund's list of its largest investments, the stocks in which the fund has invested the most dollars. Then use the Free Cash Flow Worksheet to assess several of the mutual fund's largest stocks. This is a good way to get a sense for what kinds of companies the fund managers like. Are the fund managers' favorite stocks compatible with the investor's preferences? Sure, this approach will take some time. But it enables the Free Cash Flow investor to subject mutual funds to the same analysis used for individual stocks. Investors should look at their mutual funds' largest investments periodically to make sure they're still comfortable with the fund managers' largest investments. If all this sounds like too much work, index funds are probably the best bet. Index funds are a good option because of their low expenses and because they require relatively little time to choose and monitor.

FREE CASH FLOW AND BONDS

While the Free Cash Flow Worksheet was developed for equity analysis, it can also be used to assess the creditworthiness of a debt issue. The same cannot be said of a GAAP analysis. Free Cash Flow focuses on the primary concern of the bond investor: Will the company pay interest and repay principal as scheduled? The projection period can easily be extended to satisfy the bond investor's time horizon by adding projection columns in the Worksheet. Also, the debt service ratio formula can be revised to exclude dividends.

FREE CASH FLOW AND THE FINANCIAL CRISIS OF 2008

Free Cash Flow captures a company's ability to generate cash from its operations. The Free Cash Flow Statement captures Revenues, the Operating Cash Flow Margin and capital utilization. The Free Cash Flow Worksheet enables the investor to analyze a company's historical Free Cash Flow Statements and deployment trends. Using the Free Cash Flow Worksheet in combination with an established due diligence discipline, the investor can assess the likelihood of a company satisfying the investor's return objective and can compare the most likely return with that of alternative investments.

The Financial Crisis of 2008 has stimulated a heightened appreciation for public companies' cash flows, their business models' dependence on the financial markets for debt and equity as well as their ability to pay dividends. These are subjects that are right up the alley of the Free Cash Flow investor. The Free Cash Flow investor can easily identify, on the one hand, those companies that require outside capital to grow, and on the other hand, those companies whose business models' do not need outside capital to grow. The Free Cash Flow investor also appreciates the impact of dividends on investor return but understands that dividend yield must be integrated with other sources of return in order to assess the prospects for overall investor return.

But crises come and go. Investing styles rise and fall. Investment topics heat up and then cool off. The Free Cash Flow investor is relatively immune to the ever-changing investing fads and fashions because the Free Cash Flow investor is focused on all of the major variables that affect investor return. Let others over-emphasize one or two variables and ignore the complete picture of investor return. We welcome our unfair advantage and believe it will help us find great stocks.

Equations

CHAPTER 1: INVESTING 101

$$\text{Return on Investment} = \frac{\text{Annual Free Cash Flow}}{\text{Investment}} \tag{1.1}$$

$$\text{Investment} = \frac{\text{Annual Free Cash Flow}}{\text{Required Return}} = \frac{\$10 \text{ million}}{20\%} = \$50 \text{ million} \tag{1.2}$$

$$\text{Price} = \frac{\text{Annual Free Cash Flow}}{\text{Buyer's Required Return}} = \frac{\$10 \text{ million}}{18\%} = \$55.6 \text{ million} \tag{1.3}$$

$$\text{Price} = \frac{\text{Annual Free Cash Flow}}{\text{Buyer's Required Return}} = \frac{\$11 \text{ million}}{18\%} = \$61.1 \text{ million} \tag{1.4}$$

$$\text{Free Cash Flow per share} = \frac{\text{Annual Free Cash Flow}}{\text{Number of Shares}} = \frac{\$10 \text{ million}}{10 \text{ million}} = \$1 \tag{1.5}$$

$$\text{Free Cash Flow per share} = \frac{\text{Annual Free Cash Flow}}{\text{Number of Shares}} = \frac{\$11 \text{ million}}{10.5 \text{ million}}$$
$$= \$1.05 \tag{1.6}$$

$$\text{Free Cash Flow per share} = \frac{\text{Annual Free Cash Flow}}{\text{Number of Shares}} = \frac{\$11 \text{ million}}{11.5 \text{ million}}$$
$$= \$0.96 \qquad (1.7)$$

CHAPTER 2: THE ACCOUNTING FOG MACHINE

$$\text{Current Ratio} = \frac{\text{Current Assets}}{\text{Current Liabilities}} \qquad (2.1)$$

$$\text{Working Capital} = \text{Current Assets} - \text{Current Liabilities} \qquad (2.2)$$

$$\text{Return on Equity} = \frac{\text{Annual Net Income}}{\text{Shareholders' Equity}} \qquad (2.3)$$

$$\frac{\text{Current Year's Accounting Income (Loss)}}{\text{Stock Par Value} + \text{Paid-in Capital} + \text{Prior Years' Net Income (Loss)}} = ?$$
$$(2.4)$$

CHAPTER 4: THE FREE CASH FLOW STATEMENT

$$\text{Operating Cash Flow} = \text{Net CFO} +/- \Delta\,\text{WC} = \$67,970 + \$5,000$$
$$= 72,970 \qquad (4.1)$$

$$\text{Cash Op. Costs} = \text{Revenues} - \text{Op. Cash Flow} = \$500,000 - \$72,970$$
$$= \$427,030 \qquad (4.2)$$

$$\text{Operating Cash Flow Margin} = \frac{\text{Operating Cash Flow}}{\text{Revenues}} = \frac{\$72,790}{\$500,000} = 15\% \qquad (4.3)$$

$$\text{Free Cash Flow per share (FCS)} = \frac{\text{Free Cash Flow}}{\text{Number of Shares}} = \frac{\$48,470}{20,000} = \$2.42$$

(4.4)

$$\text{Free Cash Flow Yield} = \frac{\text{Free Cash Flow per share}}{\text{Stock Price}}$$

(4.5)

$$\text{Free Cash Flow Yield} = \frac{\text{Free Cash Flow per share}}{\text{Stock Price}} = \frac{\$2.42}{\$38} = 6\%$$

(4.6)

$$\Delta \text{ Share Value due to Operations}$$
$$= \frac{(\text{Next Year's FCS} - \text{Current Year's FCS})}{\text{Current Year's FCS}}$$
$$= \frac{(\$2.70 - \$2.42)}{\$2.42} = 12\%$$

(4.7)

$$\text{Price Earnings Ratio (PE)} = \frac{\text{Stock Price}}{\text{Earnings per share}}$$

(4.8)

$$\text{Earnings Ratio} = \frac{\text{Earnings per share}}{\text{Stock Price}}$$

(4.9)

$$\text{Free Cash Flow Yield} = \frac{\text{Free Cash Flow per share}}{\text{Stock Price}} = \frac{\$2.70}{\$33} = 8\%$$

(4.10)

CHAPTER 5: FREE CASH FLOW DEPLOYMENT

$$\text{Acquired Company's Contribution to Acquirer's FCS}$$
$$= \frac{\text{Acquired Company's FCF}}{\text{Acquirer's Number of Shares}} = \frac{\$4 \text{ Million}}{20 \text{ Million}} = \$0.20 \text{ FCS}$$

(5.1)

$$\Delta \text{ Share Value due to Acquisition} = \frac{\text{Acquired Company's FCS}}{\text{Acquirer's FCS}}$$

$$= \frac{\$0.20}{\$2.42} = 8\% \tag{5.2}$$

Δ Share Value due to Operations and Acquisition

$$= \frac{\Delta \text{ in Operations' FCS} + \text{Acquired Company's FCS}}{\text{Acquirer's FCS}}$$

$$= \frac{(\$0.28 + \$0.20)}{\$2.42} = \frac{\$0.48}{\$2.42} = 20\% \tag{5.3}$$

$$\text{Number of Shares Purchased} = \frac{\text{Amount Deployed for Buybacks}}{\text{Stock Price}} \tag{5.4}$$

$$\text{Number of Shares Issued} = \frac{\text{Amount Received from Shares Issued}}{\text{Stock Price}}$$
$$\tag{5.5}$$

Estimated Number of Shares Outstanding at End of Year

= Prior Period's Number of Shares Outstanding

− Number of Shares Purchased + Number of Shares Issued (5.6)

Estimated Δ in FCS Due to Δ in Number of Shares

$$= \frac{\text{Estimated Free Cash Flow}}{\text{Estimated Number of Shares at Year-End}}$$

$$- \frac{\text{Estimated Free Cash Flow}}{\text{Prior Period's Number of Shares}}$$

$$= \frac{\$54 \text{ Million}}{19.8 \text{ Million}} - \frac{\$54 \text{ Million}}{20 \text{ Million}} = \$2.73 - \$2.70 = \$0.03 \text{ per share}$$

$$\tag{5.7}$$

Δ Share Value due to Δ in Number of Shares

$$= \frac{\text{Net } \Delta \text{ in Number of Shares}}{\text{Prior Period's Number of Shares}} = \frac{200,000}{20 \text{ million}} = 1\% \quad (5.8)$$

$$\text{Dividend Yield} = \frac{\text{Dividend}}{\text{Stock Price}} = \frac{\$1.50}{\$38} = 3.9\% \quad (5.9)$$

Δ in Debt = Free Cash Flow + Other Sources of Cash − Deployments

$$(5.10)$$

$$\text{Estimated } \Delta \text{ in Debt per share} = \frac{\text{Estimated } \Delta \text{ in Debt}}{\text{Number of Shares}}$$

$$= \frac{(\$15 \text{ million})}{19.8 \text{ million}} = (\$0.76) \text{ per share}$$

$$(5.11)$$

$$\Delta \text{ in Share Value due to } \Delta \text{ in Debt} = \frac{\Delta \text{ Debt per share}}{\text{Stock Price}} = \frac{(\$0.76)}{\$38} = 2\%$$

$$(5.12)$$

CHAPTER 6: THE FREE CASH FLOW WORKSHEET

Incremental OCF per \$1 of Additional Revenue

$$= \frac{2006 \text{ OCF} - 2005 \text{ OCF}}{2006 \text{ Revenues} - 2005 \text{ Revenues}} = \$0.33 \quad (6.1)$$

$$\text{Reinvestment Return} = \frac{\text{Incremental OCF}}{(\Delta \text{ Working Capital} + \text{Capex})} \quad (6.2)$$

$$\text{Operating Cash Flow} = \text{Revenues} \times \text{OCFM} = \text{B33} \times 0.21 = \$4,809.0$$

$$(6.3)$$

$$\frac{\text{2007E FCF}}{\text{2007E Number of Shares}} - \frac{\text{2007E FCF}}{\text{2006 Number of Shares}}$$

$$= \frac{\text{B84}}{\text{B109}} - \frac{\text{B84}}{\text{C109}} = \frac{\$2,895.7}{1,234.8} - \frac{\$2,895.7}{1,251.7} = \$0.03 \qquad (6.4)$$

Δ Share Value due to Δ Number of Shares

$$= \frac{\text{Net } \Delta \text{ in Number of Shares}^* - 1}{\text{Prior Period's Number of Shares}} = \frac{-16.9^* - 1}{1251.7} = 1.3\% \quad (6.5)$$

$$\text{Dividend Payout Ratio} = \frac{\text{Dividends Paid}}{\text{Net Income}} \qquad (6.6)$$

$$\frac{\Delta \text{ Share Value due to } \Delta \text{ Operations' FCS}}{\text{2006 FCS}} = \frac{\text{B136}}{\text{C131}} = \frac{\$0.19}{\$2.13} = 8.8\%$$
$$(6.7)$$

$$\text{Return Multiple} = \frac{\text{Investor Return}}{\text{Treasuries' Yield}} = \frac{\text{B145}}{\text{B151}} = \frac{14.1\%}{3.0\%} = 4.7 \qquad (6.8)$$

CHAPTER 7: SIX COMPANIES

$$\text{Return on Equity} = \frac{\text{Net Income}}{\text{Shareholders' Equity}} \qquad (7.1)$$

CHAPTER 9: FINDING GREAT STOCKS

$$\frac{\text{Equity Portfolio}}{\text{Maximum Loss}} = \frac{\$400,000}{\$25,000} = 16 \text{ Stocks} \qquad (9.1)$$

McDonald's Income Statement

CONSOLIDATED STATEMENT OF INCOME

IN MILLIONS, EXCEPT PER SHARE DATA	*Years Ended December 31, 2006*	*2005*	*2004*
REVENUES			
Sales by Company-operated restaurants	$16,082.7	$14,726.6	$13,755.2
Revenues from franchised and affiliated restaurants	5,503.7	5,105.9	4,838.8
Total revenues	21,586.4	19,832.5	18,594.0
OPERATING COSTS AND EXPENSES			
Company-operated restaurant expenses			
Food & paper	5,349.7	5,004.9	4,698.2
Payroll & employee benefits	4,185.4	3,860.4	3,586.5
Occupancy & other operating expenses	4,006.6	3,709.2	3,403.2
Franchised restaurants-occupancy expenses	1,060.4	1,021.5	1,002.7
Selling general & administrative expenses	2,337.9	2,167.1	1,939.1
Impairment and other charges (credits), net	134.2	(28.4)	281.4
Other operating expense, net	67.1	105.3	145.0
Total operating costs and expenses	17,141.3	15,840.0	15,056.1
Operating income	4,445.1	3,992.5	3,537.9
Interest expense—net of capitalized interest of $5.4, $4.9 and $4.1	402.0	356.1	358.4
Nonoperating income, net	(123.3)	(38.0)	(21.2)
Income from continuing operations before provision for income taxes	4,166.4	3,674.4	3,200.7
Provision for income taxes	1,293.4	1,088.0	923.2
Income from continuing operations	2,873.0	2,586.4	2,277.5
Income from discontinued operations (net of taxes of $96.8, $11.4 and $0.7)	671.2	15.8	1.0
Net income	$ 3,544.2	$ 2,602.2	$ 2,278.5

(Continued)

Per common share–basic:			
Continuing operations	$ 2.33	$ 2.05	$ 1.81
Discontinued operations	0.54	0.01	-
Net income	$ 2.87	$ 2.06	$ 1.81
Per common share–diluted:			
Continuing operations	$ 2.30	$ 2.03	$ 1.79
Discontinued operations	0.53	0.01	-
Net income	$ 2.83	$ 2.04	$ 1.79
Dividends per common share	$ 1.00	$ 0.67	$ 0.55
Weighted-average shares outstanding-basic	1,234.0	1,260.4	1,259.7
Weighted-average shares outstanding-diluted	1,251.7	1,274.2	1,273.7

See Notes to consolidated financial statements.
Source: From McDonald's 2006 Annual Report, page 40.

McDonald's Balance Sheet

CONSOLIDATED BALANCE SHEET

IN MILLIONS, EXCEPT PER SHARE DATA	December 31, 2006	2005
ASSETS		
Current assets		
Cash and equivalents	$2,136.4	$4,260.6
Accounts and notes receivable	904.2	793.9
Inventories, at cost, not in excess of market	149.0	144.3
Prepaid expenses and other current assets	435.7	640.2
Discontinued operations		380.0
Total current assets	3,625.3	6,219.0
Other assets		
Investment in and advances to affiliates	1,036.2	1,035.4
Goodwill, net	2,209.2	1,924.4
Miscellaneous	1,307.4	1,236.7
Total other assets	4,552.8	4,196.5
Property and equipment		
Property and equipment, at cost	31,810.2	29,482.5
Accumulated depreciation and amortization	(10,964.5)	(9,909.2)
Net Property and equipment	20,845.7	19,573.3
Total assets	$29,023.8	$29,988.8

(Continued)

CONSOLIDATED BALANCE SHEET

IN MILLIONS, EXCEPT PER SHARE DATA	December 31, 2006	2005
LIABILITIES AND SHAREHOLDERS' EQUITY		
Current liabilities		
Notes payable	$ -	$544.0
Accounts payable	834.1	678.0
Income taxes	250.9	569.6
Other taxes	251.4	233.1
Accrued interest	135.1	158.5
Accrued payroll and other liabilities	1,518.9	1,158.1
Current maturities of long-term debt	17.7	658.5
Discontinued operations		107.9
Total curent liabilities	3,008.1	4,107.7
Long-term debt	8,416.5	8,934.3
Other long-term liabilities	1,074.9	851.5
Deferred income taxes	1,066.0	949.2
Shareholders' equity		
Preferred stock, no par value; authorized – 165.0 million shares;issued – none		
Common stock, $.01 par value; authorized – 3.5 billion shares; issued – 1,660.6 million shares	16.6	16.6
Additional paid-in capital	3,445.0	2,720.2
Retained earnings	25,845.6	23,516.0
Accumulated other comprehensive income (loss)	(296.7)	(733.1)
Common stock in treasury, at cost; 456.9 and 397.4 million shares	(13,552.2)	(10,373.6)
Total shareholders' equity	15,458.3	15,146.1
Total liabilities and shareholders' equity	$29,023.8	$29,988.8

See Notes to consolidated financial statements.
Source: McDonald's 2006 Annual Report, page 41.

McDonald's ROIIC and Weighting

RECONCILIATION OF RETURNS ON INCREMENTAL INVESTED CAPITAL

"Return on incremental invested capital (ROIIC) is a measure reviewed by management over one-year and three-year time periods to evaluate the overall profitability of the business units, the effectiveness of capital deployed, and the future allocation of capital. This measure is calculated using operating income and constant foreign exchange rates to exclude the impact of foreign currency translation. The numerator is the Company's incremental operating income plus depreciation and amortization, from the base period. The denominator is the weighted-average adjusted cash used for investing activities during the applicable one- or three-year period.

Adjusted cash used for investing activities is defined as cash used for investing activities adjusted for cash generated from (used for) investing activities related to Chipotle. The weighted-average adjusted cash used for investing activities is based on a weighting applied on a quarterly basis. These weightings are used to reflect the estimated contribution of each quarter's investing activities to incremental operating income. For example, fourth quarter 2006 cash used for investing activities is weighted less because the assets purchased have only recently been deployed and would have generated little incremental operating income (12.5 percent of fourth quarter 2006 cash used for investing activities is included in the one-year and three-year calculations). In contrast, fourth quarter 2005 cash used for investing activities is heavily weighted because the assets purchased were deployed more than 12 months ago, and therefore have a full year impact on 2006 operating income, with little or no impact to the base period (87.5 percent and 100.0 percent of fourth quarter 2005 cash used for investing activities is included in the one-year and three-year calculations, respectively). Management believes that weighting cash used for investing activities provides a more accurate reflection of the relationship between its investments and returns than a simple average." (From McDonald's 2006 Annual Report, page 38.)

McDonald's ROIIC Calculations

"The reconciliations to the most comparable measurements, in accordance with accounting principles generally accepted in the U.S., for the numerator and denominator of the one-year and three-year ROIIC are as follows:

One-Year ROIIC Calculation

	Years Ended December 31, 2006	2005	Incremental Change
NUMERATOR:			
Operating income	$4,445.1	$3,992.5	$ 452.6
Depreciation and amortization[1]	1,224.9	1,220.3	4.6
Currency translation[2]			(41.2)
Incremental operating income plus depreciation and amortization (at constant foreign exchange rates)			$ 416.0
DENOMINATOR:			
Weighted-average adjusted cash used for investing activities[3]			$ 1,661.4
Currency translation[2]			12.6
Weighted-average adjusted cash used for investing activities (at constant foreign exchange rates)			$1,674.0
One-year ROIIC[4]			24.9%

[1]Represents depreciation and amortization from continuing operations.
[2]Represents the effect of foreign currency translation by translating results at an average exchange rate for the periods measured.
[3]Determined by weighting the adjusted cash used for investing activities for each quarter in the two-year period ended December 31, 2006 by applying the weightings below.

	Years Ended December 31	
	2005	2006
Cash used for investing activities	$ 1,817.8	$ 1,273.4
Adjusted for cash generated from (used for) investing activities related to Chipotle	(83.9)	219.2
Adjusted cash used for investing activities	$ 1,733.9	$ 1,492.6
AS A PERCENT		
Quarters ended:		
March 31	12.5%	87.5%
June 30	37.5	62.5
September 30	62.5	37.5
December 31	87.5	12.5

[4]The increase in impairment and other charges (credits), net between 2006 and 2005 negatively impacted the one-year ROIIC by 9.5 percentage points.

Three-year ROIIC calculation

	Years Ended December 31, 2006	2003	Incremental Change
NUMERATOR:			
Proforma operating income[5]	$4,445.1	$2,482.6	$ 1,962.5
Depreciation and amortization[6]	1,224.9	1,133.9	91.0
Currency translation[7]			(272.0)
Incremental operating income plus depreciation and amortization (at constant foreign exchange rates)			$ 1,781.5
DENOMINATOR:			
Weighted-average adjusted cash used for investing activities[8]			$ 4,328.9
Currency translation[7]			(13.1)
Weighted-average adjusted cash used for investing activities (at constant foreign exchange rates)			$4,315.8
Three-year ROIIC[9]			41.3%

[5]Share-based expense as reported in the Company's year end 2003 Form 10-K was $224.1 million after tax ($354.4 million pretax). For comparability purposes to 2006 results subsequent to adopting SFAS No. 123(R), the 2003 reported operating income of $2,837.0 million was adjusted for this proforma expense.

[6]Represents depreciation and amortization from continuing operations.

[7]Represents the effect of foreign currency translation by translating results at an average exchange rate for the periods measured.

[8]Represents three-year weighted-average adjusted cash used for investing activities, determined by applying the weightings below to the adjusted cash used for investing activities for each quarter in the four-year period ended December 31, 2006.

	Years Ended December 31			
	2003	2004	2005	2006
Cash used investing activities	$1,369.6	$1,383.1	$1,817.8	$1,273.4
Adjusted for cash generated from (used for) investing activities related to Chipotle	(77.7)	(97.8)	(83.9)	219.2
Adjusted cash used for investing activities	$1,291.9	$1,285.3	$1,733.9	$1,492.6
AS A PERCENT				
Quarters ended:				
March 31	12.5	100.0	100.0	87.5
June 30	37.5	100.0	100.0	62.5
September 30	62.5	100.0	100.0	37.5
December 31	87.5	100.0	100.0	12.5

[9]The decrease in impairment and other charges (credits), net between 2006 and 2003 benefited the three-year ROIIC by 6.7 percentage points."
Source: From McDonald's 2006 Annual Report, page 39.

Recommended Reading

Christy, George C., *Free Cash Flow: A Two-Hour Primer for Management and the Board* (Bangor, ME: Booklocker, 2006).

This book is for managers and board members who want to maximize their company's valuation. Included are six generic management reports that integrate Free Cash Flow and other financial metrics with customer, product, corporate, and peer data.

Henry, David, "Fuzzy Numbers," *Business Week* (October 4, 2004); www.businessweek.com/magazine/content/04_40/b3902001_mz001. htm.

This article is an excellent account of accounting's vulnerabilities and management opportunities to determine the EPS number.

Howell, Robert A., "Tying Free Cash Flows to Valuation," *Financial Executive* (May 2002).

In this concise but thorough discussion of the problems with GAAP and the benefits of Free Cash Flow, Professor Howell describes how Xerox's GAAP financials in 1997–1999 provided a misleading portrait of the company's financial condition.

Jackson, Cecil W., *Business Fairy Tales* (Mason, Ohio: Thomson, 2006).

The subtitle of this book tells it all: Grim Realities of Fictitious Financial Reporting. The author digs into the financial statements of Enron, WorldCom, Sunbeam, Adelphia and others. The Top 25 Signals of Possible Fictitious Reporting in Financial Statements is a prudent checklist for both EPS and Free Cash Flow investors.

Koch, Richard, *The 80/20 Principle* (New York: Doubleday, 1998).

There is a great deal more to the 80/20 principle than many people realize. Chapter 5's analysis of cost reduction and Chapter 7, "The Top 10 Business Uses of the 80/20 Principle," are especially insightful.

Koller, Tim; Goedhart, Marc; and Wessels, David, *Valuation: Measuring and Managing the Value of Companies,* Fourth Edition, (Hoboken, NJ: John Wiley & Sons, 2005).

This is a comprehensive 739-page guide for the professional investor and those individual investors who are strong in accounting. The combination of theory, definitions, formulas, and case studies is clearly written and helpful. Chapter 7 (Analyzing Historical Performance) is strong, especially the sections titled "Reorganizing the Accounting Statements: Key Concepts" and "Reorganizing Accounting Statements: In Practice." Chapter 8 (Forecasting Performance) is a good step-by-step treatment of the modeling process. The book's comprehensive coverage of the subject makes it an invaluable reference work. The extensive index is a useful resource.

Mulford, Charles W. and Comiskey, Eugene E., *Creative Cash Flow Reporting: Uncovering Sustainable Financial Performance* (Hoboken, NJ: John Wiley & Sons, 2005).

This is an excellent guide to the GAAP Cash Flow Statement and its many challenges as a source of investor information. It is a great resource for investors who are strong in accounting and who want to convert GAAP's "Cash provided from operating activities" into *sustainable* cash provided from *operating* activities. The book provides countless examples of items that do not belong in the Cash provided by operating activities section: nonsustainable items and items that really belong in the Investing or Financing sections.

Priest, William W. and McClelland, Lindsay H., *Free Cash Flow and Shareholder Yield: New Priorities for the Global Investor* (Hoboken, NJ: John Wiley & Sons, 2007).

This is an invaluable analysis of Free Cash Flow, equity valuations and interest rates, the equity markets, and globalization. The discussion of Free Cash Flow deployment is particularly illuminating. Chapter 6 (written in mid-2006) clearly identifies the three bubbles (housing, liquidity and corporate profits) that since the fourth quarter of 2007 have plagued financial markets. The authors' prescient analysis has been validated by events.

Rappaport, Dr. Alfred, *Creating Shareholder Value: A Guide for Managers and Investors* (New York: The Free Press, 1997).

Professor Rappaport is a pioneer in finance and investment analysis. This highly readable book was my introduction to non-GAAP analysis. It is recommended to all investors.

Rappaport, Dr. Alfred, "How to Avoid the PE Trap," *The Wall Street Journal Online,* (March 10, 2003).

Investors do not need to read this article if they know a stock with a PE of, say, 20 can require a higher cash flow growth rate than a stock with a PE of 30.

Reingold, Dan, and Reingold, Jennifer, *Confessions of a Wall Street Analyst: A True Story of Inside Information and Corruption in the Stock Market* (New York: HarperCollins, 2006).

What is it like to be a sell-side analyst? This book describes the challenges and the frustrations that make up the sell-side analyst's workday.

Sherman, H. David, "Time to Bury EBITDA, Pro Forma Earnings, and Stupid Cash Tricks," *Corporate Board Member* (September/ October, 2004).

Not enough can be said about the problems with EBITDA.

Notes

Chapter 2: The Accounting Fog Machine

1. Alex J. Pollock, "The Government Should Not Try to Promote 'Investor Confidence,'" American Enterprise Institute paper, April 2005.
2. Ibid.
3. Ibid.
4. Ibid.
5. David Henry, "Fuzzy Numbers," *BusinessWeek*, October 4, 2004.
6. Kenneth Wilcox, "Dealing with Sarbox," *Wall Street Journal*, June 1, 2007. Reprinted from *Wall Street Journal* © 2007 Dow Jones and Company. All rights reserved.

Chapter 3: Free Cash Flow

1. Alfred Rappaport, *Creating Shareholder Value: A Guide for Managers and Investors* (New York: The Free Press, 1997).
2. Tim Koller, Marc Goedhart, and David Wessels, *Valuation: Measuring and Managing the Value of Companies*, Fourth Edition (Hoboken, NJ: John Wiley & Sons, 2005).
3. See Note 2.
4. Vito J. Racanelli, "The Schwab Advantage," *Barron's*, November 27, 2006.
5. Ibid.
6. Ibid.
7. Vito J. Racanelli, "A Rookie Stays in Focus," *Barron's*, September 3, 2007.
8. Ibid.
9. Ibid.
10. Robert G. Hagstrom Jr., *The Essential Buffett: Timeless Principles for the New Economy* (New York: John Wiley & Sons, 2001). Copyright © John Wiley & Sons, Inc. Reprinted with permission of John Wiley & Sons, Inc.
11. FASB Staff Paper: "Summary of User Interviews, Reporting Financial Performance by Business Enterprises," prepared for a February 22, 2002, meeting of the Board.
12. Ibid.
13. Ibid.

Chapter 4: The Free Cash Flow Statement

1. Jonathan Laing, "Welcome to Sizzle Inc.," *Barron's,* December 25, 2006.
2. Ibid.
3. Vito J. Racanelli, "The Schwab Advantage," *Barron's,* November 27, 2006.
4. William W. Priest and Lindsay H. McClelland, *Free Cash Flow and Shareholder Yield: New Priorities for the Global Investor* (Hoboken, NJ: John Wiley & Sons, 2007).

Chapter 5: Free Cash Flow Deployment

1. Jeremy J. Siegel, *The Future for Investors: Why the Tried and the True Triumph Over the Bold and the New* (New York: Crown Business, 2005).

Chapter 7: Six Companies

1. McDonald's 2006 Annual Report.
2. Ibid.
3. Cheesecake Factory press release, October 23, 2007.
4. P. F. Chang's 2006 Annual Report.
5. Cheesecake Factory Presentation at Bank of America Conference, September 18, 2007.
6. Gene Epstein, "Stock Boosters Still Rule the Streets," *Barron's,* November 26, 2007.
7. Morningstar, Inc. © 2007. All rights reserved. The information contained herein: (1) is proprietary to Morningstar and/or its content providers; (2) may not be copied or distributed; and (3) is not warranted to be accurate, complete, or timely. Neither Morningstar nor its content providers are responsible for any damages or losses arising from any use of this information. Past performance is no guarantee of future results.

Chapter 8: The CEO and Investor Return

1. McDonald's 2006 Annual Report.
2. Ibid.
3. Panera Bread 2006 Annual Report.
4. Ibid.
5. Applebee's 2006 Annual Report.
6. Ibid.
7. P. F. Chang's 2006 Annual Report.
8. Ibid.
9. Morningstar, Inc. © 2007. All rights reserved. The information contained herein: (1) is proprietary to Morningstar and/or its content providers; (2) may not be copied or distributed; and (3) is not warranted to be accurate, complete, or timely. Neither Morningstar nor its content providers are responsible for any

damages or losses arising from any use of this information. Past performance is no guarantee of future results.

10. P. F. Chang's 2006 Annual Report.
11. Cheesecake Factory 2006 Annual Report.
12. IHOP 2006 Annual Report.
13. Ibid.
14. Ibid.
15. McDonald's 2007 proxy.
16. See Note 15.
17. William W. Priest and Lindsay H. McClelland, *Free Cash Flow and Shareholder Yield: New Priorities for the Global Investor* (Hoboken, NJ: John Wiley & Sons, 2007).
18. Panera Bread 2007 proxy.
19. Applebee's 2007 proxy.
20. P. F. Chang's 2007 proxy.
21. Ibid.
22. Cheesecake Factory 2007 proxy.
23. IHOP 2007 proxy.

Acknowledgments

Jordan Burkart, Ron Glatley, Ken Jensen, Jon Myers, Bill Priest, and Alice Wong have read some or all of the book. Their comments and corrections have been most helpful. I am most grateful to each of them for taking the time out of their busy schedules.

The Reconciliation table in Chapter 3 was created by Tom Liguori for my first book, *Free Cash Flow: A Two-Hour Primer for Management and the Board*. I very much appreciate his contribution.

In January of 2007, Bill Priest, CEO of Epoch Investment Partners, suggested I write a book about Free Cash Flow for investors. I am grateful to Bill for his suggestion and also for his important contributions to the Free Cash Flow discipline as both a writer and as a professional investment manager.

Andrew Christy has provided invaluable solutions to all computer hardware and software challenges. Without his help I could not have gotten past the title page.

My wife Nobuko has worked very hard so that I could take the time to write this book. Without her help and encouragement, I could not have gotten to the title page.

About the Author

George C. Christy, CFA has more than 30 years of experience in the financial markets. His experience at First National Bank of Chicago, Crocker Bank, and GE Capital included relationship management, credit administration, and credit policy positions. His design and implementation of a bank management system was featured in the *Journal of Commercial Bank Lending*. From 2000 to 2004, he was Treasurer of a plastics manufacturing company focused on cable and telephone service providers. He worked with institutional investors, lenders, investment bankers, and Wall Street analysts. He has a BA from Princeton University and an MBA from the University of Chicago. He holds the Chartered Financial Analyst (CFA) designation. He has contributed to *The Economist*, the *Financial Times, Financial Week*, and *Investment News*. He was a vice president and director of the Los Angeles Chapter of Financial Executives International and is a member of the CFA Institute, the CFA Society of Los Angeles, the Japan America Society, and the International House of Japan.

About the Web Site

The companion website for this book includes valuable tools to help expand your knowledge of the book's concepts as well as put them to practical use with your own companies. Visit www.wiley.com/go/christy where you will find the two downloadable Excel files introduced in Chapter 6:

- The Six Restaurants file has been completed using the financial data of McDonald's and five other restaurant companies.
- The Free Cash Flow Worksheet has the same format and formulas as the Six Restaurants file, but contains no company data. Use the Free Cash Flow Worksheet file to work on your own companies.

In addition, there is a link to the Reader's Forum found at http://www.OakdaleAdvisors.com/book.html. Participate in this forum with other readers of the book to exchange comments on Free Cash Flow investing as well as share ideas about your experience using the Free Cash Flow Worksheet.

Lastly, the Oakdale Advisors website contains links to other useful resources, as well as the author's upcoming speaking schedule. Once you have explored these online resources, please post comments and suggestions on the Reader's Forum.

Index